THE CONVENT OF CHRIST, TOMAR

THE CONVENT OF CHRIST, TOMAR

PAULO PEREIRA

SCALA

MINISTÉRIO DA CULTURA

INSTITUTO DE GESTÃO
DO PATRIMÓNIO ARQUITECTÓNICO
E ARQUEOLÓGICO

First published in 2009 by Scala Publishers Ltd
Northburgh House
10 Northburgh Street
London EC1V 0AT

ISBN: 978 1 85759 383 9

10 9 8 7 6 5 4 3 2 1

AUTHOR
Paulo Pereira
Text translated from the Portuguese by Isabel Varea

EDITORIAL CO-ORDINATION
Manuel Lacerda (IGESPAR, I.P.)
Miguel Soromenho (IGESPAR, I.P.)
Sandra Pisano (Scala Publishers)

EDITORIAL ASSISTANCE
Dulce de Freitas Ferraz (IGESPAR, I.P.)
António Ferreira Gomes (IGESPAR, I.P.)

PICTURE RESEARCH
Dulce de Freitas Ferraz (IGESPAR, I.P.)

DESIGN
Nigel Soper

Printed in Spain

ACKNOWLEDGEMENTS
The author wishes to thank Dr. Jorge Custódio for revising the text and making the necessary changes. Special
thanks go to Dr. Miguel Soromenho, Dr. Dulce de Freitas Ferraz, António Ferreira Gomes, the photographer
Henrique Ruas (IGESPAR, I.P.) and to Luís Pavão, the photographer who should really be considered as co-author.

PHOTOGRAPHIC CREDITS
All photographs by Luis Pavão in collaboration with Carlos Sá except:
Henrique Ruas (IGESPAR, I.P.) pages 47, 50, 51, 54 (bottom), 64, 65, 66 (top right), 73, 91, 92, 107 (top), 108, 109;
Teresa Gambo (IGESPAR, I.P.) page 41;
photographic reproduction by Henrique Ruas (IGESPAR, I.P.) pages 58 (right), 60 (bottom), 75

Plans: © IGESPAR I.P./DIED

Previous page
Exterior of the Charola

CONTENTS

FOREWORD

The Convent of Christ in Tomar is one of Portugal's most impressive monuments. Combining history with exceptional scale and the changing architectural styles of more than six centuries, as well as its associations with the Knights Templar, this great religious complex attracts visitors with many different interests. History, art and legend merge in the story of its origins and the events that have influenced its development.

It is here, too, that we find some of the most eloquent icons of Portuguese architecture – the Romanesque Charola, the famous Manueline window, the João III Cloister, the Chapel of Our Lady of the Conception – all of which secure the convent a place in the popular imagination. Moreover, its geographical location in the centre of the country links it to other major monuments and sites that are part of Portugal's national heritage. This book, produced by the Institute for the Management of Architectural and Archaeological Heritage (IGESPAR), in cooperation with Scala Publishers, provides an essential guide for those wishing to explore the Convent of Christ. At the same time, it offers an original interpretation of the historical and artistic forces that have helped to shape this extraordinary place.

Elísio Summavielle
Director of IGESPAR

Level 3

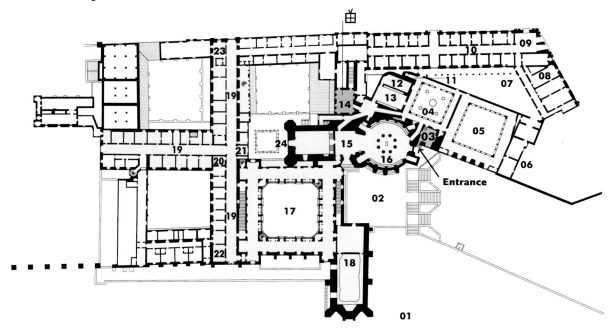

Tickets
Gift shop
Café
WC
Temporary Exhibitions
Documentation Centre

Areas open to visitors

N   0   25

01. Gardens, orange grove and
      vegetable gardens
02. Courtyard
03. Former Chapel of Saint George
04. Cemetery Cloister
05. Laundry Cloister
06. Prince Henry's Quarters (ruins)
07. Apothecary Courtyard
08. Apothecary
09. Surgery (called the 'Knight's Surgery')
10. Infirmary
11. Portocarreiros Chapel
12. Treasure Strong House
13. New Sacristy
14. King's Room
15. Main body of Church (nave and choirs)
16. Charola

17. Main Cloister
18. Chapter House (Friars and Knights)
19. Main Dormitory
20. Calefactory
21. Crossing Chapel
22. The Prior's Residence
      (16th-17th century)
23. The Prior's Residence (18th century)
24. Manueline Window
25. Santa Barbara Cloister
26. Hospedaria Cloister
27. Registry
28. Attendant's Quarters
29. Guest House
30. Novitiate
31. Novitiate Rooms
32. Novitiate Chapel

33. Refectory
34. Kitchen
35. Crows' Cloister
36. Former Library or Scriptorium
37. Cryptoportico Balcony
38. Aqueduct
39. Study Room
40. Entrance to the Crows' Cloister
41. Oil Storage Room of the
      Conde de Tomar
42. Lavatories
43. Micha Cloister
44. Oven House
45. House of the Procurator
46. Mews and Stables
47. Cistern
48. Philippine Entrance Lodge

Level 2

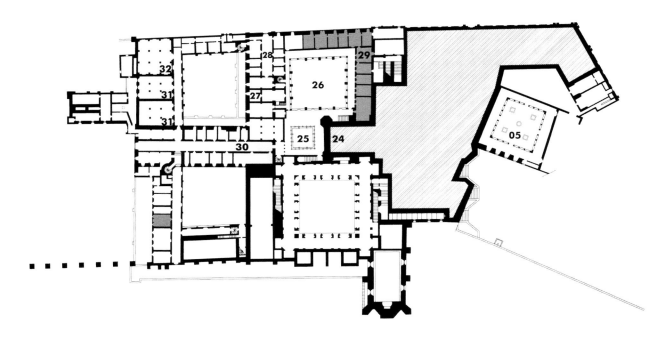

Level 1

Exit

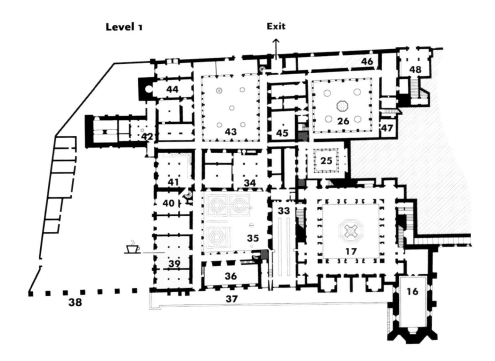

INTRODUCTION

The Convent of the Knights of Christ is one of Portugal's most remarkable monuments. Standing at the top of the hill which dominates the town of Tomar, it is composed of buildings – or remains of buildings – dating from the Roman period to the eighteenth century. The convent provides a remarkable illustration of the various chapters in the history of Portuguese architecture. The Romanesque is represented by the castle, its extensive surrounding walls and the great Charola – or Rotunda – that was the original Templar church. The Gothic influence can be seen in the fifteenth-century additions, specifically the cloisters and palaces built by Prince Henrique, better known as Henry the Navigator. The Manueline, that uniquely Portuguese version of the Late Gothic, is illustrated by the choir and sacristy commissioned by King Manuel I at the beginning of the sixteenth century. The Early Renaissance is featured in groundbreaking fashion in the hugely complicated construction of the convent itself, a monastic enclosure with six cloisters, built following the establishment of the Order of Christ in 1529. The High Renaissance and Mannerism find expression in the Great Cloister, built in the second quarter of the sixteenth century (1562) and considered by many historians to be one of the world's great architectural masterpieces. 'Plain' Classicism is evident in the simpler but more functional additions from the time of Philip III.

Quite apart from the extraordinary architecture, many significant figures have passed through and spent time here over the years. Among them were Tomar's true founder, the Provincial Master of the Order of the Temple in Portugal, Gualdim Pais, and Henry the Navigator, Administrator of the Order of Christ, which after a relatively smooth transition replaced the Order of the Temple in Portugal. Another illustrious visitor was Manuel I, who set about reshaping not only the Order but also the Avis dynasty and the convent itself. It was here that King João III developed much of his taste for architecture, the Convent of Christ becoming his favourite construction project, while Philip II of Spain clearly had symbolic reasons for establishing here the court which recognised him as ruler of Portugal.

With its historic and artistic riches, the Convent of Christ, and the area beyond the town and its environs, has played a significant part in the history and mythology of Portugal. Located practically at the country's geographic centre, from its earliest days the convent was associated with the mysteries of the Templars, Rosicrucians and neo-Templars and with the Order of Christ and its esoteric connections, which exerted a powerful influence over the fortunes and prosperity of the kingdom. With its hidden treasures – real or intangible – and legendary stories, the religious architecture of the Convent of Christ is rich in often deeply enigmatic and highly controversial symbolism. More recently, it featured in Umberto Eco's novel, *Foucault's Pendulum*, which was enthusiastically received by a sophisticated intellectual readership. Chapter 67, which describes the narrator's excitement on first seeing Tomar, opens with a quotation from the Portuguese philosopher, Sampayo Bruno, another figure who loved to explore great mysteries: 'Of the Rose let us say nothing for the moment...'

View of the 'lower
town' – the present
town of Tomar

TOMAR

It is uncertain exactly when the town of Tomar first appeared on the banks of the River Nabão, and early chroniclers mix historical accounts with testimonies that owe more to myth than to fact. We know for certain that a major Roman settlement once occupied the site of present-day Tomar, extending along a bend in the river and dominated by the castle. Many relics of the Roman era have come to light, some found by chance, others uncovered during archaeological excavations.

In fact, what stood here was probably the town of Sellium, mentioned in the third-century *Itinerary of Antonino*, a likelihood borne out by accounts dating from the time of the Emperor Augustus and by the discovery of a sizeable forum laid out in the classic style. This theory is also supported by the original name of the oldest of the town's churches, Santa Maria do Olival, formerly known as Santa Maria do Selho. This suggests that at one time there was a larger urban development on the left bank of the river. As for the town's present name, this seems to have arisen without explanation, taking on different forms with the passage of time, such as 'de Thomar' or 'Thomaris', and finally Tomar.

Possibly the names of the settlements on either side of the river also changed over the course of history. Sellium became Nabantia or Namba, when the region was under Visigoth rule and, later, documents in medieval Latin dating from the twelfth and thirteenth centuries mention Thomar, Tomaris or Thomarium.

The real founding of Tomar is, however, inextricably linked to the foundation of the castle in the first area of the region to be settled. Nevertheless, there is no doubt that a fortified village, albeit a modest one, stood on the hill in the Visigoth period and during the subsequent Muslim occupation. But it was the Templar castle, re-established in 1160 by Gualdim Pais, Grand Master of the Order of the Temple, which had the greatest influence on the development of the region. With the colonisation of the surrounding area, the town grew in the thirteenth century, expanding beyond the protection of its twelfth-century walls, while the 'lower town' gradually grew up in the valley. This village which sprang up, possibly by accident in part, in a strategic position close to the river boasted no distinctive features, apart from the church of Santa Maria do Olival – or Santa Maria de Tomar. Nothing survives of the original church, probably a modest construction, but the thirteenth-century building remains virtually unchanged today.

The church of Santa Maria do Olival enjoyed a special status. Indeed, after the conquest of Lisbon and following the reorganisation of the bishoprics, the Templars relinquished ecclesiastical rights over all the churches in Santarém and its neighbouring area. Meanwhile, the Bishop of Lisbon gave up ecclesiastical rights over all the churches in what was known at the time as the 'territory of Ceras', which included Tomar. As a result, the churches in this region became independent of the bishopric and directly answerable to the Pope, and the district was raised to the rank of diocese, with the church of Santa Maria do Olival as its see. When the east bank of the Nabão was declared *nullius diocesis* (belonging to no diocese) it was necessary to build a church, which, in the days of the Order of Christ, would serve as the mother church for parishes overseas. It was in this church that Gualdim Pais, the first Portuguese member of the Order of the Temple and close friend of King Afonso Henriques, was buried in 1195. His tombstone, along with those of other Masters of the Order, is now in a side chapel, following alterations carried out in the sixteenth century.

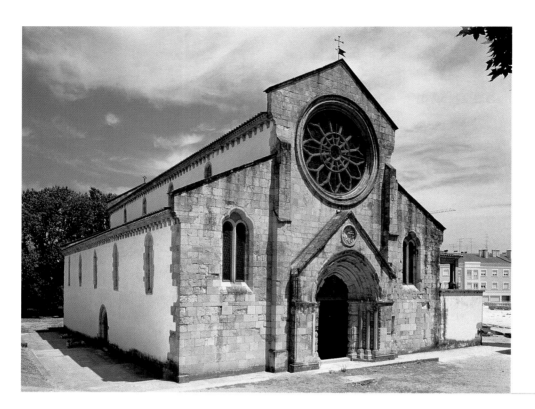

Church of Santa Maria
do Olival, Tomar

Detail of the pentalpha
(or pentagram)
inscribed on the tablet
above the central
doorway of the church
of Santa Maria do Olival

Although altered and refurbished in the sixteenth century and restored again in the twentieth, the church, which was probably completed around 1250, is distinctive in that it marks a 'split' in the Gothic style. The shape of the chancel, the slender windows and rib-vaulted roof of the apse lend the interior a luminosity and transparency never previously seen. Still more light floods in through the clerestory along the central nave and through the exceptionally large rose window. The church, whose three aisles are divided into five sections with two additional chapels set slightly back on either side of the apse at its eastern end, also has a series of very simple columns. Although relatively slender, these are sturdy enough to support the wooden roof, accentuating the lightness and Gothic quality of the building. The façade also testifies to an innovative approach, not only in the size of the rose window, which almost reaches the edges of the upper section of the wall but also in the striking configuration of the portal set within a triangular gablet. Above the entrance doorway is a circular multi-lobed tablet containing a relief of Solomon's Seal, a symbol associated with the Knights Templar.

With the growth of the 'lower town' – the original nucleus of the present town, which was newly built in the mid-fourteenth century to a standardised plan, like a French *bastide* – it became necessary to rebuild the ageing Church of São João Baptista. John the Baptist was one of the Templars' favourite saints. The church underwent a complete renovation that amounted to rebuilding, the work beginning at end of the fifteenth century and finishing in 1510, during the reign of Manuel I.

The church has three aisles divided into five sections. The chancel is rectangular, elongated to include several additions, including the sacristy and a large side chapel to the north. The façade of the church is divided into three sections, the tallest rectangular middle section crowned by linkwork, with a circular

Church of São João
Baptista, Tomar

window at its centre. The focal point of the façade is the portal with its ogee arch, framed by a rectangular gable decorated with rosettes, in a display of the 'flamboyant' Gothic style that predated the full flowering of the famous Manueline. Inside is a magnificent collection of sixteenth-century Portuguese paintings. Although the series, which concentrates on the themes of the Eucharist and the life of John the Baptist, is probably incomplete today, it is still relatively easy to interpret. Experts attribute the large, recently reconstructed, triptych to a Flemish hand – Quentin de Metsys is one possibility. It depicts the Baptism of Christ by St John the Baptist, flanked by the Marriage at Cana and the Temptation. On the back of these two panels, St John the Evangelist is depicted in *grisaille*, carrying a chalice from which a winged serpent emerges (representing the 'poison' used in the attempt to kill to him) and Saint Andrew with his cross, another saint to whom Templars frequently addressed their prayers. Other later paintings, attributed to the studio of Gregório Lopes and presumed to date from between 1538 and 1539, are exhibited on the church walls. Some have Templar themes or relate to John the Baptist, such as Salome presenting the head of St John the Baptist, and there are others depicting the Last Supper, the Communion of the Apostles, the Mass of Saint Gregory the Great, the Israelites receiving manna in the desert, and Abraham and Melchizedek. The first are inspired by the New Testament and by the eucharistic miracle at the Mass of St Gregory, while the others take their inspiration from the Old Testament. Both relate directly to the Eucharist or to biblical events that prefigured the Eucharist – the triptych includes the Marriage at Cana. A further strong Templar connection is seen in the depiction of Abraham's encounter with Melchizedek. Melchizedek (the name means 'King of Justice') is one of the most important figures in the Bible, and was particularly, although not exclusively, revered in the western Hermetic tradition as a symbol of universality. He was also regarded as a repository for the sources of the religions of the Book and hence of major importance to Christianity, Judaism and Islam. When, as 'King of Salem', he meets Abraham, he offers him bread and wine, and blesses him, so assuming the status of 'priest-king', a mythical figure associated with visions of the coming of the Messiah who, like John the Baptist, foreshadows Jesus as Messiah. The church's patron saint is the main figure in this impressively coherent group of paintings, also referred to by the overall title of *The Traveller*.

Interior of the
Synagogue of Tomar

Tomar's synagogue, the best preserved in the whole of Portugal, testifies to the way in which different faiths were able to live peacefully side by side. Built in the middle of the fifteenth century, the building is now hidden behind an unobtrusive façade, so that it looks like an ordinary house. It is constructed on a rectangular ground plan and the roof is a groin vault supported on four slender columns. The flattened capitals are decorated with plant motifs, and the oriental-style or Palaeo-Christian references on their upper parts reflect a transitional period in Portuguese architecture when the vocabulary of the early Renaissance was gradually superseded by that of the Gothic. Light entered through narrow windows in the side walls and the entrance was through a door with an ogee arch, now located in an adjacent room. Following the expulsion or forced conversion of the Jews in 1497, the Synagogue was used as a prison. It later became a small chapel dedicated to St Bartholomew and was even used as a barn. In 1939 it was bought by Samuel Schwarz and, later, the Museu Luso-Hebraico Abraão Zacuto (the Portuguese-Jewish Museum) was established here.

THE ORDER OF THE TEMPLE

THE TEMPLARS

The Order of the Temple was founded in Jerusalem in 1118 by Hugues de Payens, a cousin of St Bernard of Clairvaux, with Godefroi de Saint-Omer and seven other knights as co-founders. The intention was to protect Christian pilgrims making their way to the Latin Kingdom of Jerusalem in the Holy Land. Although its intended aim was primarily defensive, it soon became a vital part of the strategy of maintaining Christian domination in the East. The Order set up its headquarters on the site of the Temple of Solomon – where the Al-Aqsa Mosque now stands – the members calling themselves Knights of the Temple. Thus, the House of God was established in what was regarded at the time as the centre of the Christian world.

The enthusiasm which greeted the creation of the Order reflects the importance of the military and religious role it was destined to play. As St Bernard wrote in *De Laude novae militiae* (1130): 'We hear that a new kind of chivalry has risen on earth, and that it has risen on the very region of it which the rising Son Himself, present in flesh, once visited from on high... A new kind of chivalry, one ignorant of the ways of the ages, which fights a double fight equally and tirelessly, both against flesh and blood and against the spiritual forces of iniquity in the heavens'. In 1127, as the Order grew apace, Hugues de Payens, encouraged by St Bernard, travelled to Rome with five companions to seek papal support for the Order. On 13 January 1128, the papal legate, Matthew of Albano, and the abbot of Cîteaux, Etienne de Harding, were among those present at the Council of Troyes. The first, rather severe Rule of the Order was then drawn up in Latin, based on a hierarchical structure reflecting that of twelfth-century society. The combatants – or warrior-monks – were knights of noble origin who took a vow of chastity and poverty. The sergeants and shield-bearers were recruited from the middle and lower orders, and the religious duties were carried out by priests. The hierarchy was clear: knights, sergeants and shield-bearers constituted the militia, which was subject to the organisational and territorial discipline of the Order. In 1139, the French version of the Rule was completed and the Templars received the endorsement of Pope Innocent II in the papal bull, *Omne datum optimum*.

The Order expanded rapidly, especially in the West, where its military function went hand-in-hand with the farming of land by the commanderies – or monastic houses – which sprang up all over France. With the fall of St John of Acre in 1291 and the consequent defeat and abandonment of the Kingdom of Jerusalem, the Templars concentrated more on administering the revenue from their many holdings. Only in Portugal and Spain did they continue with their specifically military activities.

In Portugal, it seems likely that the Templars were still involved in combat around 1125 in the region then known as the Condado Portucalense. Documents exist recording the donation in 1128 of lands at Soure – together with the old castle which the Templars renovated – by Teresa of León, and of various endowments from her son, King Afonso Henriques in 1143 and 1159. In 1145, Afonso's brother-in-law, Fernão Mendes, had given Longroiva Castle to the Order. The help of the warrior monks proved invaluable during the conquest of Santarém in 1147. Grand Master Hugo Martonio, who led the Order when military operations began, was succeeded by another Portuguese, Gualdim Pais. Meanwhile, the Templars increased their holdings across Portugal, founding churches at Ega and Redinha, and castles at Pombal,

Tomar and Almourol. By around 1250, the lands owned by the Order extended throughout central and inner Beira and to some parts of Trás-os-Montes in the north east.

View of the citadel at Tomar rising above the great scarp

THE TRAIL OF THE TEMPLARS

The Templars' 'banking' activities – something of a novelty at the time – began when pilgrims setting out for the Holy Land and wishing to avoid the risk of robbery would leave their valuables with the Order for safekeeping. In exchange, depositors were given a written pledge – a kind of cheque in the form of a bond or bill of exchange. This was then handed to a commandery in the Holy Land, where the bearer could then withdraw the specified sum. So it was that the Templars came to manage enormous assets, which financed their activities in the East, despite the fact that they were merely guardians rather than owners. This, along with the power of the commanderies and the effectiveness of the protection offered by their military activities, made the French monarchs increasingly wary of the Knights of the Temple. Moreover, since the reign of Philip II of France, the Templars had been entrusted with the Royal Treasury, which was kept at the Temple – their fortified house in what is now Paris's third *arrondissement*.

The power of the Order was considerable, and the kings of France called upon the Templars for help

Palace built in the time of Henry the Navigator, with ruins in the foreground and a distant view of the castle keep

in times of financial difficulties, although negotiations were rarely free of problems. The warrior-monks became increasingly unpopular, a situation that was not improved by their tax-collecting activities during times of political turmoil; one example was the upheaval following the defeat of Philip the Fair in 1302, when extra funds were needed to pay for the continuing wars in Flanders. A popular mythology grew up around the Templars, another factor that helps to explain the accusations made against them during the trial that led to their abolition.

In one of the most impressive 'police operations' ever staged, Philip the Fair managed to crack the apparent impenetrability of the Templars. On 13 October 1307, the king ordered his troops to place all the Templars under house arrest in their commanderies. Apart from sealed orders sent to bailiffs throughout the country a month before, the operation had been kept absolutely secret. This may or may not explain the lack of any resistance by the Templars. Philip the Fair had his closest advisers, all of them legislators, with him in Paris, the most notable among them being his chancellor Guillaume Nogaret. The event had immediate repercussions throughout France and the Templars were publicly accused of indulging in perverted conduct – such as sodomy – and of committing various crimes 'against religion', including the adoration of idols and the use of obscene and anti-Christian rituals. On 14 October, the accusations against the Templars were set out in the document *Rex Jubet Templarios Comprehendi*, based on vague statements and various allegations of heretical or deviant practices. The accusations listed in the

documentation were: a) denial of Christ; b) denial of the Cross; c) forced and consenting acts of homosexuality; and d) adoration of an idol – allegedly a goat-headed devil figure, famously known as 'Baphomet'. These accusations, later backed up by confessions extracted under torture, were of the kind that always circulate in the popular media, especially when there is an anti-clerical mood abroad. Furthermore, the secrecy with which the Order operated and its vast accumulated wealth, both associated with usury in the popular imagination, did little to help its cause. The then Pope, Clement V, whose enthronement had been brought about by the machinations of Philip the Fair, and who later moved to France to escape the Roman papal court and palace conspiracies, helped the monarch along by issuing a papal bull, the *Pastoralis preeminentie*, on 22 November, ordering the imprisonment of all Templars. The inquisitorial process ordered by the Pope, but already compromised by the interrogations carried out by investigators working for the king, began on 8 August 1309 at the Monastery of Saint Geneviève in Paris. On 2 May 1312, despite statements in their defence given by over 500 Templar monks, the Order was suppressed. The leaders of the Order were brought before three cardinals and found guilty of various crimes. Sentence was passed on 18 March 1314, in front of the cathedral of Notre Dame de Paris. The accusation was read and, despite protesting their innocence and that of the Order as a whole, Jacques de Molay (Grand Master), Hugues de Payraud (Visitor of France), Geoffroy de Charnay and Geoffroy de

Segment of a 17th-century arch within the ruins of Henry the Navigator's palace

The ground floor of the Laundry Cloister showing a collection of stones of the Order of the Temple and other archaeological remains from the town of Tomar

Gonneville were immediately condemned to be burnt at the stake as 'relapsed heretics'.

In Portugal, however, things were altogether different. Having received Clement V's papal *Regnum in Coelis*, dated 12 August 1308, King Dinis appeared to be in no hurry to initiate the necessary procedures. As a result, the Portuguese trial was slow in getting under way. A tribunal consisting of Bishop João of Lisbon and a doctor of law, João das Leis, found nothing worthy of censure. However, the Pope had to be obeyed. On 27 November 1309, a royal decree was finally issued, ruling that all Templar possessions be placed under the protection of the Crown but should remain 'suspended'. King Dinis and King Fernando IV of Castile immediately agreed that if the Order was to be suppressed the property of the Temple would remain 'reserved'. The King of Aragon adopted a similar policy in 1311.

THE ORDER OF CHRIST

Soon after the suppression of the Order, King Dinis founded the Order of Christ, in reality a continuation of the former Order. The then Pope, John XXII, gave his consent in the papal bull, *Ad ea exquibus*, of 14 March 1319. All the knights and possessions of the original Order were thus transferred to the newly created Order of Christ, which set up its headquarters in the castle at Castro Marim in the Algarve. In 1357, the headquarters were moved to the castle at Tomar, returning to the place where it had all begun. The transfer of Templar property to the Order of Christ (and to the Order of Montesa in Aragon) meant that the activities of the former Order could safely continue in Portugal. Indeed, there was little to distinguish the new Order of Christ from the old Order of the Temple. The Military Order of Jesus Christ (*Ordo Militiae Jesu Christo*) carried the same meaning as the original Order of the Temple (*Comilitionum Christi*), in other words the Knights of Christ, referred to in the prologue to the Templar Rule drawn up at the Council of Troyes. Similarly, the monks still wore the same habit, and the insignia itself – the cross potent – was only slightly altered by inscribing a white Greek cross inside it. The ends of the cross were later modified to create the rounded cross pattée, the well-known Cross of Christ. With Manuel I at the head of the Order, the Cross of Christ soon became synonymous with the monarchy and, along with the monarch's badge of office, the armillary sphere was incorporated into the Portuguese Royal Coat of Arms. Thus the foundation of the Order of Christ amounted to the re-foundation of the Order of the Temple. Compared to the rest of Europe, it was in Portugal that the most unusual arrangements were made to maintain Templar property and continue the work of the Order. Members were subject to the Cistercian Rule, and Gil Martins, Master of the Order of Avis, which had also adopted the Cistercian Rule, was appointed Master. It was decided that the monks of the new Order should elect their own master on the death of Martins. The Abbot of Alcobaça was appointed spiritual head of the Order of Christ.

On 11 June 1321, a meeting of the chapter at Tomar adopted the rule of another chivalric Order – the Order of Calatrava – to serve as the Rule of the Order of Christ; disagreements on disciplinary and spiritual matters would be resolved according to its rules. From 1417 onwards, after the Order had seen seven Masters in office, the post was filled by members of the royal household, appointed by the Pope and carrying the new title of Governor and Administrator. The first appointee under the new regime was Henry the Navigator who, by all accounts, continued the Templar philosophy, shaping the Order of Christ in such a way as to keep alive the chivalric and crusading spirit. Under his leadership, the Order embarked on what appeared to be its true mission, namely voyages of discovery and the conquest of Asia, financed from the Order's own coffers.

In 1529, during the reign of João III, the internal organisation of the Order, dating back to the days of King Dinis, with its warrior-monks (or *Milites Christi*) and friars, was reformed to create a strictly cloistered Order. There was a clear separation between knights and friars, and it became a contemplative, monastic and completely closed Order inspired by the Rule of St Benedict. Such far-reaching changes demanded the construction of the 'new' Renaissance convent as an extension to the medieval monastery and fortress. The castle remained as the only evidence of the Templars' original military purpose.

Interior of the church of
Santa Maria do Olival

TOMAR CASTLE

The castle was rebuilt after it was decided to abandon plans to build a fortress at nearby Ceras, on the site of a former Roman *castrum*. It was, at the time, one of the biggest defensive fortifications ever built on Portuguese territory, indicating not only the size of the project but also the importance of the Order of the Temple and the entrepreneurial nature of Gualdim Pais. He was the driving force behind the building of this and other castles, including Pombal and Almourol, two of the most important (of the many) controlled by the Order. The plan was based on principles which Gualdim had observed in the advanced military architecture of the Holy Land, where he had spent five years fighting in several fierce campaigns north and south of the Kingdom of Jerusalem.

Work at Tomar began on 1 March 1160. There is ample evidence that this date is accurate, both in contemporary documents recording diplomatic activity and in the eloquent inscription, now partly obliterated, on the door leading into the *alcáçova* – or citadel: 'IN : EM : C : LX : VITI : REGNANTE : ALFONSO: /

Aerial view of the Convent of Christ, with the citadel and castle keep in the foreground

ILLVSTRISSIMO : REGE : PORTUGALIS : DOMNVS : / GALDINVS : MAGISTER : PORTVGALENSIVM : MILITVM : TEMPLI : / CVM : FRATRIBVS : SVS: PRIMO: DIE : MARCIL : CEPIT : HEDIFICARE : / HOC CASTELVM : NOMIE: THOMAR : QVOD : REX : / OBTULIT : D.......'. Translated, it reads: 'In the year of 1198 [1160 AD], in the reign of Afonso, most illustrious king of Portugal, Gualdim, master of the knights of the Temple, with his friars, began on the first day of March to build this Castle, called Tomar which, on completion, was offered by the king to God and to the knights of the Temple...'.

The great military complex consisted of the citadel, the ultimate defensive fortification; the castle with its keep; the *almedina*, the uppermost part of the fortified town whose great perimeter walls were designed to shelter, enclose and protect the population; and the town and its main square.

Tomar Castle: Porta do Sol (Sun Gate)

THE CITADEL AND ALMEDINA

The way into the citadel, the first part of Tomar to be populated, was through the Porta de Santiago (St James's Gate), a fifteenth-century addition to a barbican built during the same period. Rising to the right is the great crag topped by the terrace of the *alcáçova*. Extending to the left are the walls of the fortified town, a notable feature of which is the scarp, a Templar innovation in military architecture. The scarp is the steep slope at the base of the wall designed to keep enemies out. The scarp at Tomar, which follows every twist and turn of the crenellated walls, is the stoutest and longest of any castle in Portugal.

The next entrance is the Porta do Sol (Sun Gate), which was the main entrance during the twelfth century, when it stood in a recess in the citadel wall, flanked by the high walls of the fortress and the town. The outer wall extends southwards at a slight angle as far as the tall tower, which became known as the Torre de Dona

Parapet walk of the *almedina* of the fortified town

Following page
The citadel walls, with small square towers at each corner, and the scarp at the base

View of the castle walls with the great scarp

Catarina (Queen Catherine's Tower) and is a redesigned version of the original. At each corner of the wall are small square towers from which defenders could use flanking fire to cover the walls. After Queen Catherine's Tower, the walls curve westwards in a double 'S' shape as far as the Clock Tower. In this south-facing section is the Porta da Almedina (Town Gate) or Porta do Sangue (Blood Gate), so called in memory of the siege of 1190 by the massed Moorish troops of Yacub al-Mansur. The population resisted and no part of the fortress was surrendered, a testament to its strength and its power to intimidate. A tombstone on the great stairway leading into the convent commemorates the siege. It bears a Latin transcription similar to that on the foundation stone, plus added details which lend it the status of a 'historical monument'. The inscription is translated into Portuguese in Roman script on another stone dating from the sixteenth century: 'ERA DE 1168 REINĂDO EL REI DÔ AFONSO GALDIM PAES MESTRE/DOS SOLDADOS POTVGUESES DO /TEMPLO CÔ SEVS SOLDADOS EM O PRIMEIRO / DIA DE MARÇO COMEÇOV A EDIFICAR ESTE CASTELO POR / NOME TOMAR O QUAL CASTELO O / DITO REI OFERECEO A DEVS E AOS / SOLDADOS DO TEMPLO — ERA 1228 / AOS / 13 DIAS DE IULHO : VEO EL REI DE MAROCOS TRAZENDO 400 U. DE CAVALO / E 500 U. DE PÉ : E CERCOV ESTE CASTELO PO 6 DIAS DESTVIV QVANTO ACH/OV FORA DOS MVROS . E AO CASTELO E AO DITO MESTRE CÔ SEVS SOLDADOS / LIVROU DEVS DE SVAS MAOS . E O MESMO REI TOPRNOV Pª. SVA PATRIA CO INVME/RAVEL DETRYMENTO DOS HOMES E DAS BESTAS — HESTE HE O LITREIRO Q/ ESTAVA SOBRE O PORTAL Q VAÍ Pª OS PAÇOS DA RAINHA E É O TRESLADO DO Litro. ABAIXO'. Translated, it reads: 'It was in the year of 1168, in the reign of king Afonso that Galdim Paes Master of the Portuguese Knights of the Temple with his soldiers on the first day of March began to build this castle called Tomar which castle the said king offered to God and to the soldiers of the temple — in 1228 on the 13th day of july: the king of Morocco arrived with 400 cavalry and 500 infantry: and did lay siege

The castle keep

to this castle for 6 days and halted outside the walls, and god delivered the castle and the said master with his soldiers from their hands, and this king returned to his homeland having lost countless men and beasts – these are the words inscribed above the entrance door to the palace of the queen and were transferred to the inscription below'.

The circular structure is another tall tower which was part of the sixteenth-century restorations, known since the nineteenth century as the Torre da Condessa – or Countess's Tower. Originally, a scarp extended along the entire wall. During these same alterations, the walls were completely dismantled, although the course along which they ran can still be seen beside and beneath the chapter house, which was commissioned by Manuel I but was never completed and is now in ruins. The walls are thought to have continued as far as the Charola – the original Templar oratory – which backed onto the walls, although another theory maintains that the Charola stood apart from the walls.

When Manuel I commissioned the choir and a new doorway, and increasingly so when work began on the huge convent, the walls running westward and northward were removed stage by stage or absorbed into the new buildings.

THE MEDIEVAL FORTRESS

The medieval fortress is built on an almost triangular ground plan. Its walls, which appear unusually high when viewed from the outside, are dominated by the keep, nearly 20 metres tall, originally constructed to leave a clear space between it and the outer walls of the enclosure. Around it are the ruins of various other buildings, specifically a castle governor's palace, successively renovated during the fifteenth, sixteenth and seventeenth centuries. Later restorations were left unfinished.

As is evident from its wall facings, the keep is built of ashlar masonry cut to order but also from countless fragments of stones from earlier constructions, including several Roman tombstones. The most significant and the most eloquent of these, bearing the words 'GENIO / MVNICIPI', lies at the bottom corner of the west side of the tower. It is the remains of an altar dedicated to the guardian spirit of the town and was intended to be used as the foundation stone of the castle. It is also an obvious reference to the ancient Roman settlement and to the benevolent spirit that protected it. In other words, its *genius loci*.

Roman votive altar as the foundation stone of the castle and keep, with the inscription dedicated to the *genius loci*

General view of the
Charola, with the walls
of the medieval palaces
in the foreground

THE TEMPLAR CHAROLA (OR ROTUNDA)

THE ROMANESQUE ROTUNDA (12TH AND 13TH CENTURIES)

The famous Charola of the Convent of Christ is among the most original and emblematic examples of Templar architecture. The interior of this mighty cylindrical building is laid out in a circle to create a broad ambulatory, following the pattern of many other such buildings associated with military religious Orders, especially the Order of the Temple. The central core stands on an octagonal ground plan; the central drum also has eight sides which are then divided into 16 panels on the outer walls supported by tall, solid buttresses. Two of these wall panels were removed during the extensions of the Manueline period. The first floor is lit through Romanesque-style window slits. Close examination of the exterior shows, however, that the Charola was not all built at the same time. The two distinct types of facing – small stones up to the first floor, dressed stone above – clearly indicate two different stages of construction. The first would have begun during the last quarter of the twelfth century and continued until about 1190, when work was probably interrupted by serious skirmishes between the Portuguese and Almohad troops during the siege at Tomar. The second stage would have taken place when the church was nearing completion, around 1250. This later phase seems to have included not only the first floor of the outer walls but also the barrel vault above the ambulatory, as well as the staircase set in the wall leading to the lantern. This was destroyed by lightning in 1509, an event documented in the illuminated manuscript pages of the *Leitura Nova*, the collection of official documents instigated by Manuel I.

Above the ambulatory a barrel vault roof is supported by semicircular transverse arches surrounding the central drum. The Romanesque capitals are decorated with human figures and animal or plant motifs, and probably came from the workshop of a stonemason who may also have worked on Coimbra Cathedral. The decoration is beautifully executed, and the subjects – hybrid animals or dragons confronting birds – suggest the conflict between good and evil in the human soul and between secular and spiritual life.

Much Romanesque and Gothic religious architecture of the twelfth and early thirteenth century seems to have had a clear, common aim: to emulate the Church of the Holy Sepulchre or the Mosque of Omar in Jerusalem, both of which were circular. In those days, the terms 'imitation' or 'copy' did not necessarily mean a faithful reproduction of the original. It was more a matter of reproducing one or two basic characteristics of the model building to create the same symbolic effect. Moreover, the reference to Jerusalem, the Holy City from which the architect deliberately sought inspiration, was also an allusion to the origins of the Order of the Temple, whose headquarters were in buildings believed to be the remains of the Temple of Solomon. To the medieval mind this was always a circular structure, like the Mosque of Omar or the Dome of the Rock. The architecturally more complex Anastasis, or Holy Sepulchre, with its centrally-planned interior and circular ambulatory, was another source of inspiration for what became the fashion in religious buildings throughout Europe. But without a doubt, the Order of the Temple was one of the communities which used this model most systematically.

Completed in the thirteenth century, the Charola had an eastern door, which was in use until the Manueline reformation. In the fifteenth century, the large lantern (which has since disappeared) had a roof of glazed blue tiles and an upper drum with openings all the way around it to let the light in. A single

Interior of the Charola

fresco is all that remains of the most ancient wall decorations. Although it has not yet been closely studied, the gigantic figure of St Christopher, which is still visible on one of the panels of the blind arches along the outer wall of the Charola, is thought to date from the end of the fourteenth century.

The first alteration was made to the Charola when Henry the Navigator was governor of the Order of Christ. Two sections on the west side were opened up to accommodate a small structure to serve as choir and tribune. It is likely that the strange wooden organ pipe which is still fixed into the west side of the Charola also dates from this period.

The ambulatory
of the Charola

The triumphal arch
and the central drum
of the Charola

Paintings on a panel in
the Charola (studio of
Jorge Afonso?), c.1510:
Christ and the Centurion

THE ROTUNDA IN THE TIME OF MANUEL I

Large-scale works begun at the Convent of Christ under the auspices of Manuel I (1495–1521) in 1510 radically changed the appearance of the Charola.

In 1515, during work on the new choir on the west side, the openings in two of the Charola wall's 16 sections – in the space now occupied by a large triumphal arch – were enlarged to create a chancel facing eastwards. The former, east-facing entrance was blocked off at around this time. The Charola's opulent furnishings and decoration, the gilded ceiling ribs, the many polychrome elements and the stucco decorations added to windows and walls, transformed the building into a veritable jewel case. Tempera

Paintings on a panel in the Charola (studio of Jorge Afonso?), *c.*1510: *The Resurrection*

Manueline
ornamentation on the
cornice of the Charola's
central drum

paintings on the upper section of the walls of the inner drum depicting the instruments of martyrdom, others on the outer walls, some of which refer to Christ's Passion and others to the Sufferings of the Virgin Mary, and the magnificent panels filling the blind arches in the middle section, are believed to have been commissioned from the studio of court painter, Jorge Afonso (1475/80–1540).

Seven of the original 14 painted panels remain, each one measuring approximately 2.5 x 4 metres. The surviving paintings show episodes from the Life and Passion of Christ; it can be assumed that the number 14 was probably chosen to coincide with the 14 Stations of the Cross. However, the episodes still visible in the blind arches – although not necessarily in their original order – are The Ascension of Christ, The Entry into Jerusalem, Christ and the Centurion, The Raising of Lazarus and The Resurrection. The Baptism of Christ is incomplete, while only a fragment remains of the panel dedicated to the Pentecost.

Further additions to the Rotunda's rich iconography also included the images carved in wood by the Flemish sculptor, Olivier de Gand and his assistant, Fernão de Muñoz, which are to be found above the consoles and below the baldaquins at the corners of the arches of the inner drum of the Charola. The dome of the Charola – probably rebuilt after the lightning strike that destroyed the lantern in 1509 and which added new urgency to the project – was decorated with braided plasterwork with a central boss in gilt and blue. Most of the Manueline images which appear in the interior of the Charola seem to be in their original positions. In the recesses around the drum, arranged in what art historians call typological opposition (i.e. Old Testament 'types' appear close to, but subordinate to, New Testament 'antitypes'), there is St Gregory and St Jerome, St Peter and St Anthony, St John the Baptist and St Paul, St Basil and St Ambrose (or St Augustine) and also St Dominic. On the inside are the Crucifixion, the Saints and Doctors of the Church, along with Old Testament prophets on the other, heralding the coming of the Saviour.

The wall paintings of the central drum, which are presumed to be those commissioned by Manuel I from Fernão Anes (active 1511–21) from 1510 onwards. However, some experts attribute them to Fernão Rodrigues, painter in residence at the convent between 1533 and 1562, since this was probably the period from which the original paintings – and the most recent repaintings – date. They show 16 of the instruments of Christ's Passion, supported by angels – a series which has much in common with that

Two figures, arm-in-
arm, in plasterwork in
the Charola

appearing on medallions in the cloister of the Jerónimos Abbey of Santa Maria in Lisbon.

The predellas beneath the main panels above the altars encircling the outer wall represent St Anthony preaching to the fishes, and St Bernard. On the upper panels of the outer drum of the Charola, sometimes alternating with panels containing a window, a series of tempera paintings represent scenes from the Life of Christ and the Sufferings of the Virgin Mary. These are attributed to the Mannerist painters,, Simões de Abreu and Domingos Serrão, and are thought to date from between 1592 and 1600, although they may have been repainted over earlier paintings of the same subjects.

Mural in the vault of the
Charola, with sections
showing royal heraldry
and architectural motifs

Mural in the vault of the
Charola, with sections
showing royal heraldry
and architectural motifs

The paintings on the vaulted ceiling of the Charola also date from the Manueline period and were only recently uncovered, some during scientific investigations, others when whitewash was removed from the ceiling. The presence in one of the sections of the Manueline armillary sphere, opposite the shield bearing the coat of arms of Queen Maria, suggests that this group dates from between 1510 and 1518. It appears that all sections of the Charola were filled with frescoes, mostly with a vermilion or crimson background, onto which were painted *trompe-l'oeil* 'architectural' motifs, originally in *grisaille*. In addition to ribs, sculpting and mouldings, the murals contain three-dimensional representations of corbels and capitals, as well as intertwined ropes. Scattered here and there are creatures such as doves, bats and monkeys, which appear to represent the struggle between good and evil. The overlap between this kind of 'narrative' architecture, with the characteristic Manueline ropes, is remarkable. Even more impressive is the intertwining of rib vaults and mouldings, with bare tree trunks and roots featured on two of the ceiling panels. In these sections the background is dark green instead of vermilion. The trunks crisscross and literally pierce the painted mouldings, as if to provide a supporting framework beneath the painted architecture. This seems to confirm the idea that the architecture of the Manueline period sought to create a kind of 'hybrid' form, in an attempt to become one with nature.

Aerial view of the
Convent of Christ
showing the monks'
infirmary, the Charola
and the two Gothic
cloisters

THE CONVENT

THE GOTHIC CLOISTERS (15TH CENTURY)

Expansion of the monastery began during the governorship of Henry the Navigator. The cloister adjoining the Charola dates back to around 1420 and its design, which drew on the flamboyant style of the Monastery of Batalha, was entrusted to Fernão Gonçalves. The master builder's signature in Gothic script – FNAM:GLZ:FEZ – appears on the base of one of the columns. The name by which it is known – the Cemetery Cloister – derives from the fact that it was intended as a burial place for the monks and senior dignitaries of the Order of Christ. In this, an addition to the pantheon at Santa Maria do Olival, the dead were laid to rest beneath the slabs under the arcade or in arcosolia (tomb niches). The surrounding buildings were altered during a construction scheme carried out by King Philip; one of them – a rectangular structure roofed by very simple intersecting pointed arches – served as the sacristy before the Manueline era.

Gallery of the
Cemetery Cloister

Twin columns in the upper storey of the Cemetery Cloister, with capitals showing plant motifs in the 'flamboyant' tradition

Base of column in the Cemetery Cloister showing the signature of Fernão Gonçalves

The New Sacristy, 1575?

Upper floor of the
Laundry Cloister

The cloister known as the Laundry Cloister was enlarged, creating a link between the Cemetery Cloister and the royal quarters, which extended as far as the last circle of fortification of the citadel (with which it shared a wall). Furthermore, it had to be adapted to accommodate the different levels between the floor of the Cemetery Cloister and the ground floor of the palace area, which was much lower. As a result, it has two storeys, although the level of some areas was raised during restorations. The lower storey, with lancet arches edged with smooth-faceted ashlar stone, draws on the Late-Gothic Mediterranean style that typified buildings of the period of Afonso V (1432–81): plain, aesthetically austere and functional. Moreover, the Laundry Cloister required a simple, functional design since it was here that the monks would do their washing and carry out other domestic tasks.

The construction of the palace also dates from Henry the Navigator's time, although little of it still survives. Following the changes made at the end of the sixteenth and beginning of the seventeenth century, its importance declined and it eventually fell into ruin.

Part of the
archaeological remains
of the Palace of Henry
the Navigator

THE MANUELINE UPPER CHOIR

The West Façade (1510–1513)

As governor of the Order of Christ, Manuel I clearly wished to boost the image of the community and the area it occupied at Tomar. In 1503, he called a General Chapter at Tomar in order to reform the rule of the Order. It seems fairly certain that from this time onwards the monarch redoubled his efforts to renovate the Order's Tomar headquarters. But he was unable to proceed with his plans until 1510, when he commissioned Diogo de Arruda to undertake the complex and wide-ranging task of constructing the choir to the west of the Charola.

Work on the choir took from 1510 until 1513. Built close to the west face of the Charola, stylistically it had no known precedent. It consisted of an upper choir to accommodate the choir stalls and a lower chamber – the sacristy proper. It would also have had a separate entrance.

The west façade of the choir is built between two large buttresses. The central axis of the window frame, topped by a circular oculus, is loaded with plant decorations and crowned with the Cross of Christ flanked by two armillary spheres. At the base is the bust of a bearded old man enclosed in a knot, which supports the roots of an oak tree on either side. This oak tree is divided into two heavy branches which extend upwards to form the window frame.

This description is firmly in line with Ramalho Ortigão's late nineteenth-century interpretation of the iconography of the façade and the window, recognised as one of the finest examples of the Manueline style. In fact, Ortigão believed that he saw represented there 'corals', 'seaweed', 'cork oaks', 'oak branches',

General view of the Manueline choir and church, 1510–15

Plan of the choir and Charola (according to Graf)

Chapterhouse window (photograph: Vigé and Plessix, Biblioteca da Ajuda)

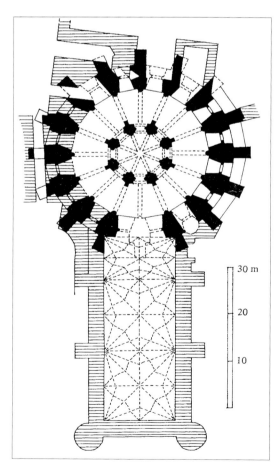

West façade of the
Manueline choir and
church, 1510–15

West façade
(photograph: Vigé
and Plessix, Biblioteca
da Ajuda)

The southernmost cylindrical buttress on the west façade

'holm oak' and 'foliage'; but also 'waves', 'bells', 'stout chains' and 'ship's ropes', 'discs' or 'cork buoys', 'large rings', 'sails (...) of a galleon'; and 'the holy tree, the tree of the Bible, the tree of Jesus, whose symbolic branch is an attribute of the Passion and of the Paschal lamb, the Glory and the Martyrdom'. This reading has inevitably contributed to the extraordinary reputation of the Manueline style while also confirming how its maritime symbolism created a direct connection with the sea. Above all, the Manueline style is a radical and extraordinary form of decoration characteristic of the Late-Gothic period, and an obvious move away from Classical and Renaissance forms.

A rope running horizontally across the façade is encircled by buoys. The outer surface of both buttresses has the realistic look of oak bark. The south buttress displays a representation of complete and slightly twisted roots immediately below a large belt fastened by a buckle. Further up, four men in

Detail of a window
moulding

Window detail: chains
and armillary sphere

At the base of the west
window, a bearded man
encircled by a knot
of Manueline rope
(according to some
traditions he is 'the
Architect', to others the
'Old Man of the Sea')

Window detail: a branch
of an oak tree, which
creates a baldaquin,
supported by a ribbon
adorned with tiny bells

Cross of Christ above
a window

armour stand on corbels, each of them carrying a coat of arms. The north buttress also has roots, this time severed, immediately below a string of broad links. On the level above – corresponding to the men in armour on the opposite buttress – are three angels bearing coats of arms. The iconography is clearly based on heraldry and symbolism. The four knights are senior heralds or, to be more precise, kings of arms, bearing the attributes that they would carry with them at royal festivities: the caduceus – a staff entwined with serpentine forms crowned by a fleur-de-lys – and the shield. The arms displayed by these knights show the royal symbols of the Order of Christ: the armillary sphere and the Cross of Christ in two different styles, in other words, the Templars' cross pattée and the variant used by the Order of Christ itself. The same arms – the sphere and the cross – are displayed by the three archangels (one of which is missing) on the side opposite the knights. While the knights stand on corbels, suggesting they have 'real' weight, the archangels have no corbels, suggesting they are flying. According to ancient heraldic tradition, their slightly inclined posture and folded garments imply that they are celestial beings, the opposite numbers of the earthly kings of arms whom they serve as heralds. The sixteenth-century heraldic text, *Tratado Geral de Nobreza*, specifically describes the rules stating that angels should be regarded as heralds and messengers. The left side of the façade therefore represents the celestial or spiritual realm, which is why the roots are severed and have no contact with the earth. By contrast, on the right-hand side of the façade, which corresponds to the earthly realm of the knights, the roots are whole. The other symbols follow the same hierarchy. In fact, on the right – or 'earthly' side – is the insignia of the Order of the Garter, a secular Order of chivalry, created and governed by men. On the left – or 'celestial' side – is the chaplet, the string of beads symbolising spiritual knighthood and the dignity and devotion to the service of God of the knights of the religious and military Order of Christ, of which Manuel I was governor. Interestingly, a statue of the king at prayer at the Jerónimos Monastery, wears an identical chaplet. Similarly, at the Chapter in Tomar in 1503, when the extension of the convent was being planned, the monarch wore a round chaplet. Meanwhile, the buoys that encircle the ropes on the façade (so much a part of Manueline maritime symbolism) may well be a reference to the royal house of Avis-Beja and, more specifically, to

Manuel I's father, the Infante Fernando, who adopted the buoy as his personal emblem.

Completing this emblematic device, the trunk of the oak tree envelopes the knot and the bust of the bearded man at the base of the window. We can assume that the man is Jesse, although here he is somewhat unusually shown carrying the prophetic tree on his shoulders. More commonly, the tree is seen to sprout from the breast of the recumbent figure of an old man. Furthermore, the tree is one of the most important elements in this particular iconography in that it is the artistic expression of Isaiah's prophesy that Christ would be born from the stem of Jesse ('*Egerditur virga de radice Jese et flos a radice ejus ascendet*' – 'And there shall come forth a rod out of the stem of Jesse, and a branch shall grow from his roots'). Manuel I famously felt a special affinity with the words of the prophet Isaiah foretelling the coming of Christ, for he firmly believed that he himself was a new Emmanuel. It is unsurprising, therefore, that the tree of Jesse showing the genealogy of Jesus should figure so prominently here.

The oak tree on the west façade of Tomar symbolises the merger between the Emmanuel of the prophecies and the figure of the monarch. In his speech to the Papal Court in Rome, the Augustinian Cardinal, Aegidius of Viterbo, used a series of rhetorical devices to express this symbolic relationship and to show how the king's destiny had been determined by his name – Emmanuel – the very fulfilment of Isaiah's prophesy. Significantly, Pope Julius II was a member of the della Rovere family, and since *rovere* is Italian for 'oak', such a tree appeared on his family coat of arms.

The two empty baldachins standing on either side of the window, with outer coverings representing tree bark, were probably meant to hold images of David and Solomon, the most significant figures in Christ's genealogical tree. Hence, there is a wonderfully eloquent blend of heraldic devices and biblical symbolism which bring together the prophesies of Isaiah, the name of the monarch, the Pope and Christ himself. The speech made by Aegidius of Viterbo in 1507 was later written down and a copy reached Portugal in 1508, just two years before work began on the west façade. Thus the west façade of the Convent of Christ creates an iconographic bridge linking the Order of Christ with the figure of Jesus, whose name it bore, and with the divine status of the monarch. Christ is metaphorically represented by mouldings in the form of bare branches, breaking into blossom as they climb towards the Cross of Christ at the top of the tree. The iconography of the west façade also presents Manuel as both governor of the Order and ruler of the Empire, appointed by God to reign over both earthly and celestial spheres.

Today, the main body of the choir is sandwiched between buildings erected during the major

South window of the sacristy of the Manueline church, partially obscured by the Great Cloister

On the south window, a bearded man wearing a Phrygian cap encircled by a knot

On the north façade, a bearded man encircled by a knot

The north façade of the sacristy, later absorbed into the Hospedaria (Guest House) Cloister

Intact roots on the
south buttress

Knight on the south
buttress with royal
heraldry and armillary
sphere

Belt and buckle on
the south buttress

Angel with armillary sphere on the north buttress

programme, which culminated in the construction of the 'new' convent – the Santa Barbara Cloister to the west, the Hospedaria (or Guest House) Cloister to the north and the Great Cloister to the south. Originally, however, it was a massive structure, towering over the few houses remaining in the neighbourhood of São Martinho. On the lower floor, on the same level as the floor of the sacristy beneath the choir, there were three windows. As well as the west window, there was one to the south, which is now behind two panels of the wall of the Great Cloister. It can still be seen from the first or ground floor of the cloister. The third window was walled up, and there were no windows on the north side. Here, there was just a string cornice containing two busts, of which only one survives. It is now, somewhat mysteriously, housed in a small room in the Hospedaria Cloister.

The south window, which is not as large or as spectacular as the west window, is nevertheless a remarkable Manueline feature. At the base is the bust of a bearded man wearing a medieval barret cap – possibly a Phrygian cap – set inside a knot, similar to the one that appears on its western counterpart. The decorations on the window posts on either side seem to have been inspired by the kind of ephemeral architecture created for specific festive events: an armillary sphere, along with a ribbon wound around two bare tree trunks adorned with artichokes and topped by an urn from which flames emerge.

The interior of the choir (1513–1515/1525?)

Another building programme began around 1515, when the highly reputed master builder João de Castilho was appointed to take charge. His brief appears to have been to sort out a series of problems that Arruda had left unresolved. Castilho was commissioned to construct a link between the old Charola and the choir to the west of it. He also had to complete the roof of the nave (Castilho famously specialised in vaults) and the connection between the choir and the nave of the church. Furthermore, he was instructed to build a new entrance, sumptuous enough to convey the importance of the community and its most noble patron. In response, he created the south portal. Castilho managed to finish all this work in record time. Meanwhile, since around 1510, thanks to the monarch's generosity, the interior of the Charola had been embellished by fine liturgical furnishings and the general decorative scheme outlined earlier. The choir is a rectangular structure covered with rib vaulting divided by three panels, supported by eight load-bearing corbels, four on each wall. The corbels, with fluted extensions, each have two rows of decorations with

Rope encircled by buoys

mainly plant motifs on the lower level and skilfully executed figurative carvings above them. Light enters through four windows, two each on the north and south sides, and through a circular oculus at the west end. The choir is built above the sacristy. Access from the choir and church to the Charola is through a monumental ogival arch in a wall decorated with a further arch that follows the contours of the church, decorated with typical Manueline-style plant and animal reliefs. The keystones of the vaults are adorned with heraldic devices. One of the most interesting themes of the decoration of the choir is the appearance of the 'goblet of flowers' on the corner corbel on the left side of the end wall. This is probably a sacred symbol since the *putti* supporting it have wings, in contrast to the wingless angels on the opposite side. This distinguishes between the two allusions, one to the transcendental and celestial (the goblet), and the other to the earthly and human, namely the Cross of Christ, symbolising an Order founded by men.

The Manueline church with the door below leading to the sacristy in the crypt

This pattern, which strongly emphasises the opposition between the divine and the earthly, the spiritual and the secular, is repeated, in the same position – on the left and right – on the buttresses of the exterior of the choir. The goblet, or vessel, symbolises the Mother of Christ who, at the Annunciation, became what the litanies refer to as the 'vessel' or the 'fountain'. The idea behind the rest of the programme – and the later one for the cloister of the Jerónimos Monastery – was to correlate the symbols of Christ and the Virgin Mary with the heraldic devices of the royal house. The idea was greatly helped along by the names of the King and Queen – Manuel and Maria – and the nature of the royal coat of arms, with white lilies, the Five Wounds and the ubiquitous armillary sphere. This display of personal emblems was intended as a tribute to the building's royal patrons and a secular counterbalance to the sacred paintings on the ceiling of the Charola.

Corbel on the north wall showing the royal coat of arms supported by a mermaid

Corbel in the southwest corner showing a bowl of lilies, symbol of the Virgin Mary, supported by angels

Corbel in the northwest corner showing the Cross of Christ supported by *putti*

Corbel in the shape of bare tree trunks which begin to sprout again as they coil around the mouldings

The original sacristy is underneath the upper choir and is entered through a door cut into the wall at the base of the choir. This appears not to have been the main entrance, and the wall was probably closed up later. At the foot of the stairs, which have an up and a down flight, is a small crypt-like space beneath a flattened stone vault in typically Manueline style, whose keystone is decorated with an eight-pointed star. Here again, it is the west window that is the most remarkable. Like those on the choir's south window, the decorations on the window posts and lintel draw on motifs, such as artichokes, seen on temporary structures built for street festivals. As Paul Evin showed in a study now considered a classic, such decorations owe much to the art of *passementerie* – the creation of luxurious trimmings such as tassels, buttons, cushions and pillows. One corbel is in the shape of a cushion trimmed with small bells, an example of the use of simulacra in Manueline architecture.

Detail of the interior of the west window

The South Portal (1515)

In order to build the south portal the buttresses of the south wall had to be removed. Similarly, two external panels of the former Romanesque Charola and the small choir built in the time of Henry the Navigator were sacrificed in order to create access between the oratory and the nave of the church. The portal's iconography includes a depiction of the Virgin and Child immediately beneath the canopy. This is accompanied by other, smaller ones set on corbels and small, slender pillars. On the upper level are St Jerome and St Gregory, St Augustine and St Ambrose. Beneath them are an unidentified prophet and St John the Evangelist – the latter seemingly in the grip of an apocalyptic vision as he gazes at the sky. On the lower level, immediately above the door, there are three prophets and what many assume to be the image of Solomon. The iconography creates an obvious harmony between the New and Old Testaments, with figures and stories from each arranged in logical sequence, tracing the history of the Christian Church

The main portal
(photograph: Reynolds
and Cifka, Biblioteca
da Ajuda)

South portal: Our Lady and Child

South portal: Solomon

South portal: St Augustine and St Gregory the Great

South portal: St John the Evangelist (?)

South portal: signature of João de Castilho

South portal: decorations in the Plateresque style

South portal: armillary sphere topped with pomegranates and supported by *putti*

from the predictions of the prophets and Sibyls to the birth of Jesus and the final consolidation of the Church as an institution, here represented by the Doctors and Fathers of the Church.

Stylistically, the south portal is a mixture of Manueline and Gothic but it already shows the influence of the decorative vocabulary of the Renaissance in the form of the ornamental style known as the Plateresque – at the time, very much in vogue in neighbouring Spain. In turn, the Plateresque was based, albeit fairly loosely, on the iconography commonly seen in Italian Renaissance buildings, which were almost always 'archaeological' or 'antique' in nature, in other words 'Romanesque' or in the 'Roman style', with strange half-human creatures, medallions, goblets, chalices, strings of beads and skulls. The door posts and archivolts have two rows of typically Manueline decorations – tree trunks, *putti* playing trumpets, animals and plants, and one innovative row of Plateresque medallions and grotesques. At the base of the portal, on the right-hand post, a tablet bears the signature of the architect João de Castilho, and the date of completion, 1515: 'C A S. C OS-: 1. 515'. ('*Castilho. Construiu 1515*') – Built by Castilho 1515.

CONSTRUCTION WORK (1530–1551)

On 14 June 1529, Friar Antonio de Lisboa was appointed by King João III and the papal nuncio to draw up a new Rule for the Order of Christ. The aim was to return it to the simpler and purer values from which it had gradually drifted away. Other ancient Orders, such as the Augustinian Canons Regular of the Holy Cross of Coimbra, governed by Jeronimite monks like Antonio de Lisboa, were also in need of reform. The Order of Christ became an enclosed Order, following the new rule and statutes imposed by Friar Antonio. These were based on the Benedictine Rule but adapted in line with the new spirit of renewal. They sought to improve the way religious Orders were organised and to bring about a return to old-style monasticism. And following long years of intellectual decline, a further goal was to provide the convent with a new generation of learned monks, versed in Latin, theology and the arts. Friar Antonio chose a symbolic 12 novices with whom to found the new-style Order in February 1532. The reforms did not go

Decoration of the door transoms and tympanums showing Friar António of Lisbon, at the entrance to the chapter house in the Great Cloister, from the work of João de Castilho

Decoration of the door transoms and tympanums showing St Augustine, at the entrance to the chapter house in the Great Cloister, from the work of João de Castilho

Decoration of the door transoms and tympanums, showing St Jerome, at the entrance to the chapter house in the Great Cloister, from the work of João de Castilho

down well with the older monks, and there were expulsions that caused deep resentment but Friar Antonio's fervour for change and his Augustinian ethos won the day. According to the Jeronimite chronicler Friar Jacinto de São Miguel, transcribing words attributed to Antonio, 'the spiritual building must be accompanied by the temporal, because there is no Religion without a Convent; and this was in an almost ruined state, without dormitories, cloisters or novices, nor the workshops necessary for the subsistence of the Community due to the negligence of the old Friars'.

In a letter of 4 March 1530, João III commissioned João de Castilho, once described by the commander of the Portuguese garrison at Mazagão (now El-Jadida) in Morocco as a 'man fit to build the world', to construct a massive piece of architecture to stand alongside the medieval and Manueline buildings. It was to be a model of modernity and functionality, erected in the space to the west of the Manueline choir. The main structure adjacent to the existing convent building was based on an extremely rational concept – a large rectangle arranged around a cruciform passageway. On each side of this passageway were four cloisters – the main or Great Cloister, the Hospedaria Cloister, the Crows' Cloister and the Micha (or Bread) Cloister. To these was added the so-called Necessarias (or Latrine) Cloister – a projecting structure on the west side used only for waste disposal. A fifth cloister, the tiny Santa Barbara Cloister as it came to be known from the end of the eighteenth century, was erected to fill the remaining space between the Manueline choir and the new building. It was built on more than one level in order to make use of the difference in levels between the earlier buildings – the church and choir – and the open spaces to the west. On the lowest level were the foundations, basements and cisterns. Above, were the floors used by the monks, containing the dormitory, refectory and novitiate. Communication between floors was by means of an unusual system of staircases, some of them set in spaces between walls and many of them spiral, but all carefully organised to provide easy access to every part of the cloister.

Aerial view of the Convent of Christ showing the cruciform structure of the work carried out in the reign of João III

At the same time, the architectural vocabulary used was radically different from that favoured by Manuel I. This was avant-garde architecture. All the Manueline heraldic devices were concealed, or even removed completely, to make way for much simpler smooth and cut surfaces and rows of classically inspired columns and capitals. As the historian Rafael Moreira states, Castilho brought with him an almost immediate shift from the traditions of medieval or Gothic architecture to focusing on creating volume and space. Castilho was largely self-taught and took his inspiration from various sources. He certainly would have read Vitruvius's treatise *De architectura,* in the translation by Cesare Cesariano, as well as *De Architettura* by Leon Battista Alberti and Diego de Sagredo's *Medidas del Romano,* a work that enjoyed considerable fame at the time. It was published in Spain in 1526 and was equally successful when published in Lisbon some time after 1535. Castilho's work combined Vitruvius's principles of *firmitas*

Three-centred arches
in the Santa Barbara
Cloister

(strength), *utilitas* (functionality), and *venustas* (beauty), based on his study of Ancient Greek and Roman architecture, with the precepts of spatial harmony proposed and practised by Alberti and the traditions of the Iberian Peninsula, described by Sagredo, in which there was greater emphasis on decoration and detail. Together, they paved the way for the experimentation that characterised the Renaissance in Portugal.

THE SANTA BARBARA CLOISTER

João de Castilho's construction programme probably began with the small Santa Barbara Cloister, a cubic 'empty space' next to the lower walls of the colossal Manueline choir and church. This cloister was the precise point at which the new additions linked up with the 'old' Manueline church, specifically at the level of the cruzeiro (or crossing), which was the proposed site for the monks' cells. It is thought to have been some time between 1531 and 1532 that the architect created this cloister in miniature with three depressed arches on either side – a Plateresque form – supported on stout columns against the base of the famous west façade. The crypt-like, almost underground, lower floor was covered by rib vaulting. A simpler vaulted gallery with a depressed arch ran along the first floor but was apparently taken down on the orders Fernando II, between 1843 and 1844, so as not to obscure the Manueline window.

This little cloister, built by an architect who had taken on board some of Sagredo's ideas, brings together the Plateresque and the Late Gothic, to create a new artistic language, determined to break away from the dense, excessively ornamented Manueline style. How else can the decision be explained to partly obscure the splendid, iconic window which would continue to amaze historians for centuries to come?

Depressed arches in the Santa Barbara Cloister

Stone showing the passage of the channel of the convent's water system in the Santa Barbara Cloister

JOÃO DE CASTILHO'S GREAT CLOISTER

The Great Cloister, built between 1533 and 1545, must have been seen as a masterpiece at the time – even when it remained unfinished. It was partly dismantled and replaced by the present cloister by Diogo de Torralva (also a masterpiece), on which work began in 1558, when João de Castilho's work was still 'new'. Castilho's original cloister would have been more densely but simply designed, with the classic column-arch pattern repeated in sets of two on each side.

On each side were four sections, each consisting of a buttress and two twin arches at ground level, with a similar pattern repeated on the upper storey. A corridor running along the four sides, with staircases leading off, connected directly and indirectly with the ground-floor rooms used by the monks: the refectory, dormitory (also referred to as the cruzeiro, or crossing), and the ground floor of the unfinished chapter house. It also gave access to the Santa Barbara Cloister, which then led to the Hospedaria Cloister, the church and the choir. Part of Castilho's construction can still be seen in the corner recesses of the 'new' cloister. Two flights of stairs set inside the stout walls of the east and west sides are also part of the original construction, as is a smaller flight on the north side.

These two main staircases provided communication between the ground floor of the church and that of the cloister. On the lower floor ,at the bottom of the steps on the east side, is the monumental entrance to the chapter house. This consists of two large arches, one of which has been walled up. A third arch, at right angles to the other two, bears the inscription 'ANNO DOMINI 1545'. On the tympanum above the door, immediately opposite the stairs, is a relief of Friar Antonio de Lisboa, hands clasped and wearing the habit of the Order of Christ, with the inscription 'F. ANTº. DE LYXBOA DOM PRIOR REFORMADOR DESTE CONVENTO POR MANDADO DELREI DOM IOAM TERCEIRO' ('Fr. Antonio de Lisboa, prior, reformer of this convent by order of King João III'). On the principal door is a scene from the life of St Jerome , showing the saint in the desert with the lion, with the inscription 'DEVS PROPITIVS EST OMNI PECCATORI' ('God is gracious to all sinners'). The figure of St Augustine also appears with his attributes – the bishop's crosier and mitre. In his hands is a building representing the church and, on his head, what Rafael Moreira calls 'the biretta of a man of letters'. He is flanked by an unidentified figure and St Augustine bent over his books, and an apocryphal episode from the life of the saint – a child drawing water from the river, symbolising Faith. These doors, with their rich iconography, lead directly to the unfinished chapter house.

THE CHAPTER HOUSE

This rather odd building has still not received the attention it deserves from architectural historians. Its proportions are Manueline, while in terms of elevations it is distinctly Gothic. Work would certainly have started around 1515 and resumed in 1530, shortly after the beginning of the reforms to the convent. The upper floor, which is reached via a terrace on the same level as the church, has a Manueline triumphal arch, possibly restored, at one end. This floor, which was never completed and is open to the elements, was intended to be used by the Chapter of the Knights, who were expelled between 1530 and 1534.

Beneath it, during the building of the Great Cloister between 1533 and 1540, João de Castilho created another room – a kind of crypt. At the back is the niche which held the altar of the chapter house chapel. Strangely, the lower part of the building is more 'modern' than the upper part. This lower section was destined to be the chapter house of the monks, following the reforms of 1529. Beyond these two chapels there is an atrium forming a reception area, where an inscription at the entrance to the lower chapel dates it to 1541.

The chapter house has many features in common with its counterpart at the Jerónimos Monastery: it, too, was designed by Castilho, probably in the 1520s, and it, too, was left unfinished. It was only during nineteenth-century restorations that the chapter house was finally completed. From the outside, the distinctive Manueline or Late-Gothic character of this monumental construction, whose western side takes in part of the citadel wall, can be clearly seen. The building was probably of exactly the same proportions as the Manueline choir, church and sacristy, and configured in the same way, with a lower and upper floor.

West side of the
chapter house

Vestibule of the
chapter house

General view of
the ruins of the
chapter house

The transept

THE CRUZEIRO, DORMITORY CORRIDOR AND CHAPEL

The cruzeiro (or crossing) is another classical construction with clean, unadorned architecture and a
monumental, extremely wide, coffered ceiling in oak. The walls are lined up to halfway with seventeenth-
century *azulejos* (glazed tiles) in blue and white. The upper floor of this building and the floor immediately
below it, both in the form of a Latin cross, follow strict functional principles. Half of the total of forty monks'
cells were on the upper floor, four along the south-facing corridor, four on the north side and another 12
facing west, with the remaining 20 cells on the lower floor. Each corridor was nearly 49 metres long, in what
was the largest construction of its kind in Portugal, with connections to other rooms used by the monks
in accordance with the monastic rule: the choir and church to the north, the Great Cloister to the south
and the refectory to the west. Light enters the corridors through windows, one of which looks out onto the
west façade – to the Holm-Oak Courtyard and the wooded area known as Sete Montes and the monks'
orange orchard – while another in the middle of the west corridor looks out onto the Micha Cloister.

90   The Convent of Christ, Tomar

North gallery of
the transept

The place where the two corridors meet forms the actual cruzeiro, an interesting architectural solution thought up by João de Castilho with the assistance of Pedro de Agorreta. It is roofed, with a lantern whose dome resembles a priest's biretta (again, borrowed from the Plateresque). Decorative reliefs of garlands and *putti* provide a light-hearted touch to an otherwise extremely sober building.

At the end of the corridor running west to east is a cube-shaped space, built in 1533, which juts out into and towers above the Santa Barbara Cloister. This is a chapel which contains an image of Christ Seated or Our Lord of the Reed, a terracotta sculpture by Inácia da Encarnação dating from 1654. Set under a pre-Baroque baldachin, it occupies almost the entire space of the chapel. The ceiling is a stone barrel vault decorated with 91 stone caissons, each containing a relief, many of them quite unusual. They include a Hermes, the figure of a king or pope, a buffoon, a series of Labours of Hercules and scenes from the story of Samson and Delilah, as well as four witty episodes from what is clearly a morality tale.

Lantern above
the crossing

THE REFECTORY AND 'WINE CELLAR'

The long refectory has a barrel vault roof divided into sections by caissons, separated by quadrangular ribs and classical stone mouldings; it rests on a continuous cornice. At the far end are two windows with twin semicircular arches surmounted by two escutcheons, on either side of a niche which originally housed a panel depicting a religious subject. On each of the two longest walls, facing one another, are two pulpits dated 1535–36, one of which is accessed from inside the wall. Each is decorated with the same symbolic Renaissance motif – the figure of Eros, god of love.

From the pantry, which connects the refectory and the kitchen, a spiral staircase leads to an underground store room. Above the stairwell is what must be the most mysterious figure to appear on a keystone on a vault in the entire convent. It is a relief of the head of a mature man, bearded and wearing a turban, with three faces, one facing forwards, the other two sideways. Other three-faced and two-faced figures appear in Tomar, on capitals in the fifteenth-century church of St John the Baptist although, following the convention of the time, these are foliate masks intended to combine the figure of Old Man Winter – or the Green Man of popular myth – and Janus, the two-headed god of beginnings and endings, looking backwards and forwards to the winter and summer solstices.

The 'wine cellar' runs the length of the building, and its front wall – which once had three windows under semi-circular arches – faces the monks' orange orchard. Scholars researching the Templars' esoteric practices believe that the three-faced figure on the keystone above the spiral staircase leading to this room might indicate that it was intended as a place for Hermetic rituals and that the 'wine cellar' was simply a disguise.

Pulpits in the refectory,
1536

Vault keystone with
three-faced figure above
the entrance to the
'wine cellar'

Detail of vault keystone in the 'wine cellar'

THE HOSPEDARIA CLOISTER

The Hospedaria (or Guest House) Cloister, built between 1541 and 1542 and standing immediately to the west, still provides clues as to the style of the earlier Great Cloister – although the first storey is simpler, with architraves instead of arches. The Plateresque influence of Diego de Sagredo is obvious, particularly in the composition of the elevations.

Since it was here that visitors to the convent were accommodated, it was essential that the cloister should make a good impression on guests. It consists of four galleries, each 29 metres long, and each divided into four sections. On the ground floor, double semi-circular arches stand on columns with broad capitals, described by the Jeronimite historian José de Siguenza as 'Doric Order'. Instead of arches, the upper floor has architraves set on central, delicately curved Ionic columns, which Siguenza defined as 'Composite Order'. The elevations of the cloister are interspersed with quadrangular buttresses running from top to bottom, crowned by small cylindrical towers each with a rosette on top. The galleries on the ground floor are roofed with rib vaults, while the upper floor has a timber beam and coffered ceiling, and a tiled roof.

On its north side, the cloister had a third storey, with a ceiling lower than that above the first-floor gallery but with the same type of design – architrave and central column, with a tiled wooden roof. Some time later, the balance of the perfectly square cloister was upset by the building of more guest accommodation on the upper storey. Worse was to come during the reign of Philip II, when a cumbersome and inelegant new dormitory was added, standing on depressed arches designed to reinforce the building and distribute the weight of the upper walls.

The upper storey on the north side of the Hospedaria Cloister was demolished, along with the upper storey of the Santa Barbara Cloister. It is above this that the entrance to the unfinished corridor leading to the confessional is visible. In the quest for Renaissance perfection, the Hospedaria Cloister, like the others in the convent, was built close up and obscuring the north wall of the choir and church, studiously avoiding Manueline ornamentation. Inside one of the small cells on its upper floor, the bust of a man encircled by a rope is still visible (one of the earlier Manueline decorations). It is striking to see such a dramatic piece of iconography in such a small space.

The Hospedaria (Guest House) Cloister

Ground floor of the
west gallery of the
Hospedaria (Guest
House) Cloister

THE CROWS' CLOISTER

Similar in layout to the Hospedaria Cloister, the Crows' and Micha Cloisters are reduced versions of their more prestigious neighbour.

They were more functional spaces, intended to be used by the novices and for charity work (the word *micha* refers to the crust of bread handed out to the poor), so they were never given the perfect finishing touches accorded to the Hospedaria Cloister, although the iconography revolves around the same themes.

Inscriptions on the keystones in the rooms around the cloister reveal that it was built between 1537 and 1546. Constructed on a square ground plan, it has two corridors, each almost 29 metres in length. The lower storey is divided into four sections with double arches on stout, smooth columns containing large basket capitals, separated by a quadrangular buttress. On the upper floor, there are four closed sections, with rectangular windows with carved aprons and two continuous lintels, one above and one below the windows. The lower galleries have vaulted ceilings. This cloister would have been a hub of activity, since it gave access to the areas used by the learned members of the monastic community. The entrance to the original Prior's House was here, as was the library (which has since disappeared) and the scriptorium, from which an internal spiral staircase led up to the library and study rooms and to the learned friars' dormitory on the top floor. From 1844 until 1934, this part of the cloister was occupied by the Count of Tomar, António Bernardo da Costa Cabral and his descendants, who converted the outbuildings into the farmhouse of the Sete Montes country estate. The scriptorium was converted into an olive press and

North gallery of the
Hospedaria (Guest
House) Cloister

one of the studies into a storehouse for oil containers. The olive press was destroyed in the twentieth century in order to convert the room into the chapel of the Seminary for Missionaries.

The Crows' Cloister

THE MICHA CLOISTER

The Micha (or Bread) Cloister was also built between 1530 and 1546. An inscription on one of the keystones of the vault in the west gallery is dated 1543.

Also on the west side, on the tympanum above one of the doors leading to the outside of the convent is an inscription inside a large tablet supported by *putti*: 'IN NOMINI DOMINI / O MUI ALTO E PODEROSO E CATHOLICO REI D. JOÃO III DESTE NOME MANDOU REFORMAR E EDIFICAR ESTA OBRA NO ANNO DO SENHOR DE 1534 E SE ACABOU NO DE 1546 [3]'. Translated, it reads: 'In the name of God / the most high and mighty catholic King João III commanded that this building be remodelled and built in the year of our lord 1534 and it was completed in the year of 1546 [3]'. This was the main gate of the convent. The original main entrance occupied what is now a passage between the Cemetery Cloister and the choir and church. Rafael Moreira's theory is that the change was made because the old door was too exposed to public view.

The lower floor is divided into four sections separated by rectangular buttresses. A continuous cornice runs right round the courtyard, which has double arches on smooth columns with large capitals – a design identical to the adjacent Crows' Cloister, with similar decorations. However, each of the galleries on the upper floor is completely different from the rest. The south side is occupied by a balcony, bounded by a platband. Rising above it is the recessed wall of the new guest house built in Philip II's time, resting on depressed blind arches, as it does in the Hospedaria Cloister. At ground level, there is access to other

Lower gallery of the Hospedaria (Guest House) Cloister

functional spaces, such as the wine cellar, pantry and kitchen. A door on the east side leads to a long, wide room (the Proctor's House), the wood store with its depressed vault and the bread oven from which the cloister takes its name.

The north façade is distinguished by the large but architecturally inferior Prior's House, an addition perched somewhat inelegantly on top of the original structure. The west façade is unlike any of the other galleries within the convent's cloisters. On this side there is a covered way, or balcony, identical to the one on the south side, to which a roof was later added. Set slightly back from the courtyard, there are three separate but identical structures, with large triangular gables decorated with medallions and topped with urns and spheres.

These are the façades of what came to be known as the *Cortes* (or Courts), as it was said to be here that Philip II of Spain was proclaimed King of Portugal by the Portuguese court. Two of the three rooms were originally intended as dormitories for the novices, while the other, more architecturally complex, space was to be the novitiate chapel. They would have been built after the main renovation work, although they may also have been the result of a change to the initial plans, probably made in 1550.

At the side of the Micha Cloister is a tall structure known as the Necessárias (or Latrine) Cloister. In the middle of this courtyard is a cistern for collecting the water to flush the latrines on the same floors as the friars' and novices' dormitories and to carry waste to a cesspit which emptied close to the outer wall.

Richly decorated gables
of the Micha (Bread)
Cloister

THE NOVITIATE ROOMS

On the first floor of the Micha Cloister are three remarkable novitiate rooms. This was what contemporary documents referred to as the 'new construction', which was added to the original plans for remodelling the existing convent buildings or creating new ones.

In each of them, João de Castilho seems to have tried to emulate Vitruvius's hypostyle hall. In the first two he experimented with four central columns, with simplified versions of the Ionic capital supporting a wooden ceiling. These were the novices' dormitories, each lit by a variety of windows and two *oeils-de boeuf*, one semicircular and three rectangular, set in the end walls. The rooms may have been based on the engraving of a similar space by Cesare Cesariano – fondly referred to as an 'experiment' by Renaissance architects – in his illustrated 1511 edition of Vitruvius.

Finally, around 1549–50, in the square room which completes this floor, he built one of the masterpieces of the Portuguese Renaissance. The room is composed of 16 perfect Corinthian columns, with composite capitals, in the antique style. Only the four central columns are freestanding; the others are set into the walls.

The columns support an architrave, which in turn supports the coffered roof formed by two intersecting barrel vaults. The formal balance achieved by these almost anonymous rooms is such that they can be considered as one of the earliest and most successful examples of Renaissance architecture in Portugal. Here, it is possible to see how the concept of open space supersedes the earlier tradition established in the Middle Ages, in which space was there to be filled rather than to exist in its own right. Here, space is used in the modern sense, to create a harmonious whole.

Entrance to the Micha
(Bread) Cloister

Dormitory corridor in
the novices' quarters

The hypostyle hall has four central columns and 12 columns against the walls, all with standard Corinthian capitals supporting an architraved, coffered wooden ceiling. This would later be reproduced in stone in the small but magnificent Chapel of Our Lady of the Conception.

Dormitory corridor
showing the flattened
vault

First hall of the
novitiate rooms

The novices' chapel

Following page
The novices' chapel

The Latrine Cloister, the
projecting structure on
the convent's east side

The present form of the
Great Cloister

THE GREAT CLOISTER (OR JOÃO III CLOISTER)

João de Castilho's time at the Convent of Christ was followed by another remarkable architectural event
– the construction of a new Great Cloister.

No one knows for certain why King João III called a halt to the work directed by Castilho. It seems that
the cloister was deemed 'unsafe' and this was enough to force yet another series of aesthetic and stylistic
changes. Castilho's successor, Diogo de Torralva, took over at the convent in 1554. He had worked on the
Jerónimos Monastery at Belém, and the Palace of Bacalhoa, carrying on the work of the great Francisco
de Arruda, who happened to be his father-in-law.

On arriving in Tomar, Torralva, whose skill and knowledge was unparalleled in Europe, set about the
task of replacing the external structure of the earlier cloister. Begun during the regency of Queen Catarina

Upper gallery of
the Great Cloister

in 1558, the new cloister shows the architect's mastery of the language of classicism. He was clearly influenced by the Italian Mannerist architect Sebastiano Serlio's *Books III* and *IV*, and inspired by buildings such as the Villa Imperiale at Pesaro in Italy, from which he made suitable adaptations in proportions and in the use of building materials to meet the requirements of the convent.

He used the same formal classical vocabulary for his cloister, at the same time as embracing High-Renaissance developments in architecture. On the upper storey he created a connection between the lower part of the support for a Serlian (or Palladian) arch and the central arch framed by architraves supported on two columns. Unusually, on the lower storey, Torralva duplicated the pilasters. Following the pattern set by Vitruvius, two classical orders are used here: Ionic above, and Doric below.

Lower gallery of
the Great Cloister

The Great Cloister seen through the arches on the upper floor

Columns on the upper floor of the Great Cloister

Following pages
Spiral staircase in a corner of the Great Cloister

Spiral staircase of
the Great Cloister

Spiral staircase of
the Great Cloister

The south façade,
where it joins the
Tomar aqueduct

The result is a structure of diaphanous transparency, matching the delicate, pliant 'Augustinian' luminosity of its predecessor, further enhanced by the soft, warm colour of the stone. The ribbed galleries (whose 'ribs' are purely for effect), with rectangular ashlar keystones decorated by reliefs, combine with double walls formed by architectural motifs that appear enlarged, as if forming part of a stage set. The walls are broken up by apertures and windows of various types – *oeuils-de-boeuf*, mirrors or transoms – in a manner never seen before on the Iberian Peninsula. Were it not for its vast dimensions, the cloister might be taken for an architect's scale model. And it is no accident that the qualities of light and shade are accentuated by the interplay of the yellow limestone of the outer surfaces, and the black – or rather, grey – marble of the recesses.

The sheer size and scale of the spaces and supporting elements in the cloister are remarkable. They are accentuated by an example of truly Mannerist inventiveness – the cylindrical staircases set in the inner corners of the cloister, leading up to the terrace. The spiral balustrades glimpsed through the windows lighting the staircase lend a jewel-like quality to a purely functional structure.

The scholarly Torralva would also have applied his knowledge and experience to another part of the convent: the south façade, where it meets the aqueduct, with its impressive base of faux rough-hewn stone of the kind favoured by Serlio. This part of the building has attracted little attention from art historians and was probably completed by another distinguished architect, Filippo Terzi, or possibly by Pedro Fernandes de Torres.

This cloister conceals another Manueline window, identical in form to its more famous counterpart in the chapter house. Here, the decorative motifs are inspired by public celebrations such as bonfires, and include stylised branches bound with ribbons. It is most evident in this part of the convent how much architects during João III's time were determined to move away from overly ornate Manueline decoration – either covering it, or walling it up. Such excesses must have seemed outmoded and absurd to those accustomed to the elegant simplicity of Classicism. Besides, by this time, the Portuguese people were no longer interested in the message it carried.

SEVENTEENTH-CENTURY IMPROVEMENTS

There are further contrasts between the Great Cloister and the additions to the north wing of the Hospedaria Cloister made under Philip I and Philip II. These additional buildings included the new dormitory, the Sala dos Reis (or Kings' Hall) and adjoining rooms and, most notably, the so-called New Vestibule, an austere structure attributed to Diogo Marques Lucas and built in 1620.

A broad and undistinguished structure extending westward and built in the reign of Pedro II, between 1688 and 1690, served as the convent's infirmary. Despite its overall stylistic simplicity, the Sala dos Cavaleiros (or Knights' Hall), situated in the corner of the building, is striking. According to ancient oral tradition, it was here that the blessing of the Knights took place. The room is square, with an octagonal wooden ceiling and deep windows, and was probably used as a surgery. It connects with the corridor of the infirmary and the convent's large dispensary, whose work is alluded to in the painted ceiling decorations, which show medicinal plants and have pharmaceutical and even alchemistic references.

João de Castilho obviously devoted a great deal of thought to the design and construction of the convent's colossal water system but to make up for the inadequate quantities that accumulated in the large tanks he provided, a supply of water had to come from remote sources. Unfortunately, this supply only became available in the surrounding area in 1617, and to the convent itself in 1619, during the reign of Philip II.

Work began at the end of the sixteenth century. The necessary purchase of land for the installation of the system was first documented in 1595, during the reign of Philip I. It was designed by the royal architect Filippo Terzi, who was in charge of work at the convent during this period, but completed under the supervision of Pedro Fernandes de Torres.

The aqueduct collects water from several sources in a wide humid valley to the north of the convent. It is six kilometres long, with some stretches running completely or partially underground, and the remainder crossing a monumental bridge. The most elegant section of the aqueduct – possibly the most impressive of any in Portugal – is in the Pegões Valley. Here, standing between steep slopes on either side of a very deep valley, the structure consists of a long series of arches on two levels, which are set at an angle, further adding to its grandeur. The arches on the lower level, where the slope is steepest, are – somewhat unexpectedly – pointed. This section continues for nearly 220 metres. On top of these arches stand 58 lower, but no less impressive, circular arches supporting the channel carrying the water. The other arcaded sections are in the next valley; 34 semicircular arches are complemented by a further series of 18 and 13 arches that link to two water sources with cupolas and decanting basins. The most spectacular part of the structure is the point where it reaches the convent itself; it enters via a series of 21 massive arches which finally converge with the walls of the convent's south façade.

Interior of the Chapel
of Our Lady of the
Conception

THE CHAPEL OF OUR LADY OF THE CONCEPTION

This chapel is one of the jewels of the European Renaissance and deserves a guidebook to itself. Standing halfway up the hill that leads westward from the town to the convent, it is attributed to João de Castilho and his assistant Pedro de Agorreta. It was built under the patronage of the reformer of the Order of Christ, Friar Antonio de Lisboa and, almost certainly, that of King João III himself. Diogo de Torralva put the first of the finishing touches to the chapel, and the work on the top of the building was completed by Filippo Terzi. The main façade features a triangular pediment above a rectangular central door, with a small architrave flanked by two rectangular windows with cutaway embrasures. There are two side doors – north and south – with small triangular pediments, and four windows on each side. The chancel is rectangular. The church has a gabled roof over the nave, with a small terrace above the chancel, and is crowned by a circular structure with a tiled dome. A flight of stairs leads to a turret on the terrace. Seen from the outside, the transept protrudes slightly, with pilasters to distinguish it from the rest of the side of the building. It is topped by a triangular pediment with a narrower base than the one on the façade. Each pediment has a half oculus level with the cornice, and the pilasters are topped by Ionic-order capitals. The interior is extraordinarily refined.

The proportions of the east end of the chapel, which includes the chancel, are based on the golden rectangle principle. The space is subdivided into three aisles, a transept and chancel, using two rows of columns with cylindrical shafts and Corinthian capitals. The impressive series of architraves set on these columns defines the spatial hierarchy of the interior, as well as supporting the barrel vaults above the aisles and transept. The alternating caissons and lozenges on the ceiling are decorated with typical High-Renaissance motifs. The chancel is roofed by a hemispherical vault reminiscent of an egg shell, and above the crossing is a dome. Here in the chapel, Castilho replicated in stone the wooden vaults which he had experimented with two years earlier in the novitiate rooms at the convent. He also managed to resolve, in a quite remarkable way, the major problem with Renaissance architecture inspired by the Ancient World. The challenge was to create a church façade modelled on that of a Roman temple with a triangular pediment and to organise the internal space to accommodate three aisles in a rectangular box, which had to be of equal height.

There is plenty of support for Rafael Moreira's theory that the building was intended to be a funerary temple for João III and his wife Queen Catarina. His hypothesis is based on a passage in a text by Fernão Duarte de Montarroio, which states that the king wished to be buried at Tomar. However, there was no royal will to substantiate this wish. The tombs would have lain in the transept, on either side of the chancel. The symbolism of the temple relates to death, with the dome above the transept serving as a metaphor for the cosmos, with four stone masks – possibly representing the four winds – at each corner. One of the two capitals depicts a skull, (symbol of death) and a phoenix (symbol of immortality) turned towards the nave. Another shows bean pods, a further funerary symbol since, according to Ancient Roman tradition, beans were the food of the dead. On the outside, the dome is topped by spheres or balls of fire, and an egg – the cosmic egg, whose shell appears to be represented by the vault above the chancel. Egg motifs appear in large numbers throughout the convent, symbolising birth, baptism and, in the case of the chapel, the Renaissance.

The Convent of Christ, Tomar

The Convent of Christ is a genuine compendium of Portuguese architecture. It has been and will no doubt become again the subject of other books but they would tell a different story – one inspired by the many secrets and unspoken truths that wait here to be uncovered, and by the unmistakable aura surrounding this special place – a place regarded in the sixteenth century as 'Jerusalem on earth'.

The Chapel of Our Lady of the Conception

BIBLIOGRAPHY

Aa.vv. *Atlas de Cidades Medievais Portuguesas* (coord. A.H. de Oliveira Marques, Iria Gonçalves, Amélia Aguiar Andrade), Lisbon, INIC, 1990.

ALVES, Ana Maria, *Iconologia do Poder Real no Período Manueline*, Lisbon, 1985.

ALVES, Adalberto, *As Sandálias do Mestre*, Lisbon, 2001.

ANDERSON, William, *Green Man*, London, Harper Collins, 1990.

ANES, José, 'Alquimia e Surrealismo (Alquimia, Imaginal e Surreal)' in *As Tentações de Bosch e o Eterno Retorno*, exhibition catalogue, Lisbon/Milan, 1994, pp 223-231.

AREIA, A. Vieira d', *O Processo dos Templários*, Lisbon, s.d.

ATANAZIO, M. C. Mendes, *A Arte do Manueline,* Lisbon, 1984.

AZCARTE, José Maria de, 'El tema iconográfico del selvage' in *Archivo Español del Arte*, no. 93, Madrid, 1948, pp 81-99.

BALLESTEROS, Carmen, 'A Sinagoga Medieval de Évora' in *Cidade de Évora*, no. 1, 2nd series, 1994–1995, pp 179-211.

BALTRUSAITIS, Jurgis, *Le Moyen Âge Fantastique*, Paris, 1981.

BAPTISTA PEREIRA, Fernando António, 'Notas sobre a representação do homem silvestre na arte portuguesa na arte portuguesa dos séculos XV e XVI' in *História e Crítica*, no. 9, 1982.

BAPTISTA PEREIRA, Fernando António, *Arte Portuguesa da Época dos Descobrimentos*, Lisbon, 1996.

BARBOSA, Álvaro José, *Os Sete Montes de Tomar. Recuperação da cerca do Convento de Cristo,* Lisbon, 2003.

BARBOSA, Álvaro, 'A arquitectura templária de Tomar' in *Cadernos da Tradição. O Templo e a Ordem Templária de Portugal* (dir. Manuel J. Gandra), Lisbon, 2000.

BARREIRA, João, *Arte portuguesa. Evolução estética*, Lisbon, s.d.

BARROCA, Mário J., 'A Ordem do Templo e a arquitectura militar portuguesa do século XII' in *Portugália*, New Series, vols XVII–XVIII, 1996–1997.

BARROCA, Mário J., 'Os Castles' in *Nos Confins da Idade Média* (dir. Luis Adão da Fonseca), exhibition catalogue, Brussels, Europália 91, 1991.

BARROCA, Mário J.; MONTEIRO, João Gouveia (coord. by), *Pera Guerrejar. Armamento Medieval em Espaço Português*, exhibition catalogue, Palmela, 2000.

BARROCA, Mário, 'Contribuição para o estudo dos testemunhos pré-românicos de Entre-Douro-e-Minho' in *IX Centenário da Dedicação da Sé de Braga*, vol. I, Braga, 1990, pp 101-145.

BARROS, João de, *Crónica do Imperador Clarimundo*, 2 vols, Lisbon, Sá da Costa, 1953.

BATATA, Carlos, *As Origens de Tomar. Carta Arqueológica do Concelho*, Tomar, 1997; *Batisseurs des Cathédrales Gothiques (Les)* (dir. Roland Recht), exhibition catalogue, Strasburg, 1989.

BERNHEIMER, Richard, *Wild Men in the Middle Ages*, Harvard, Harvard University Press, 1952.

BLUTEAU, Rafael, *Vocabulario Portuguez e Latino*, Coimbra, Colégio das Artes da Companhia de Jesus, 1792, (1° T), 1720 (6° T).

BONARDEL, Françoise, *Philosophie et alchimie*, Paris, 1993.

BORDONOVE, Georges, *Les Templiers*, Verviers, 1977.

BRANDÃO, Fiama Hasse Pais, *O Labirinto Camoniano e Outros Labirintos*, Lisbon, 1985.

BREDA SIMÕES, Manuel, 'Tomar. Le Temple et l'Empire du Graal' in *Les Templiers, le Saint-Esprit et l'Âge d'Or,* Lisbon, 1985.

BRUNETI, Almir dos Campos, *A Lenda do Graal no contexto Heterodoxo do Pensamento Português*, Lisbon, Sociedade de Expansão Cultural, 1974.

BRUNO, Sampaio, *Os Cavaleiros do Amor*, Lisbon, 1960.

CAMILLE, Michael, *Image on the Edge*, London, Reaktion Books, 1992.

CAMILLE, Michael, *The Gothic Idol. Ideology and Image-making in medieval art*, Cambridge, 1990.

CAPELO, José Manuel, *Portugal Templário*, Lisbon, 2003.

CHARPENTIER, John, *L'Ordre des Templiers*, Paris, 1944.

CHICÓ, Mário Tavares, *Arquitectura Gótica em Portugal*, Lisbon, 1981.

COELHO, Maria da Conceição Pires, *A Igreja da Conceição e o Claustro de D. João III do Convento de Cristo em Tomar*, Santarém, 1987.

CONDE, Manuel Sílvio Alves, *Tomar Medieval – o espaço e os homens (sécs XIV–XV)*, Tese policopiada, UNL, 1988.

COSTA, Fr. Bernardo da, *História da Militar Ordem de Nosso Senhor Jesus de Cristo*, Coimbra, 1771.

COSTA, Dalila Pereira da, *A Nau e o Graal*, Porto, 1978.

COSTA, Dalila Pereira da, *Corografia Sagrada*, Porto, 1993.

CUNHA, Rui Maneira, *As Medidas na Arquitectura. Século XIII–XVIII. O Estudo de Monsaraz*, Lisbon, 2003.

D'ORCET, Grasset, *Historie Sécrète de l'Europe*, vol. I, Paris, (republished) 1998.

DESWARTE, Sylvie, *Les Enluminures de la 'Leitura Nova' 1504–1522*, Paris, 1977.

DIAS, Pedro, *O Gótico*, vol. IV of *História da Arte em Portugal*, Lisbon, 1986.

DIAS, Pedro, *A Arquitectura Gótica Portuguesa*, Lisbon, Estampa, 1994.

DIAS, Pedro, *A Arquitectura Manuelina*, Porto, 1988.

DIAS, Pedro, *História de Arte em Portugal – o Gótico*, vol. III, Lisbon, 1986.

DIAS, Pedro, *Visitações da Ordem de Cristo de 1507 a 1510 – Aspectos Artísticos*, Coimbra, 1979; *Dios Arquitecto* (aa.vv., J.ª Ramirez, René Taylor, ª Corfboz, Robert Jan van Pelt, ª M. Reipoll), Madrid, 1994.

ECO, Umberto, *Arte e Beleza na Estética Medieval*, Lisbon, Presença, 1989.

ECO, Umberto, *O Pêndulo de Foucault*, Lisbon, 9th edition, 2002.

FERREIRA DE ALMEIDA, Carlos Alberto, 'O Românico' in *História da Arte em Portugal*, ed. Alfa, vol. III, Lisbon, 1986.

FIGUEIREDO, Fidelino de, *A Épica Portuguesa no Século XVI* (facsimile of the 1950 edition), Lisbon, 1987.

FRANÇA, José-Augusto, *Tomar*, Lisbon, 1999.

FREITAS, Lima, 'O Esoterismo na Arte Portuguesa' in *Portugal Misterioso*, Lisbon, 1998, pp 176-213.

GAIGNEBET, Claude; LAJOUX, Jean-Dominique, *Art Profane et Religion Populaire*, Paris, 1988.

GALVÃO, Duarte, *Crónica de D. Afonso Henriques*, Lisbon, s. d.

GANDRA, Manuel J., 'Alquimia em Portugal' in *Discursos e prática alquímicas, I*, Lisbon, 2001, pp 175-230.

GANDRA, Manuel J., 'Filosofia Hermética' in *As Tentações de Bosch e o Eterno Retorno*, exhibition catalogue, Lisbon/Milan, 1994, pp 117-127.

GANDRA, Manuel J., 'Terra de gigantes' in *À Descoberta de Portugal*, Lisbon, 1982.

GANDRA, Manuel J., *Dicionário do Milénio Lusíada*, vol. I, Lisbon, 2003.

GANDRA, Manuel J., *O Império do Espírito Santo na região de Tomar e dos Templários*, Lisbon, 2000.

GANDRA, Manuel J., 'O Templo e a Ordem Templária de Portugal' in *Cadernos da Tradição*, no. 1, Lisbon, 2000.

GANDRA, Manuel J., *Os Templários na Literatura* (anthology), Lisbon, 2000.

GANDRA, Manuel Joaquim, 'Os Templários' in *Portugal Misterioso*, Lisbon, 1998, pp 296-355.

GANDRA, Manuel Joaquim, *Da Face Oculta do Rosto da Europa*, Lisbon, 1997.

GOIS, Damião de, *Crónica do Felicíssimo Rei D. Manuel*, 4 vols, Coimbra, Imp. da Univ., 1949–1954.

GOMES, Pinharanda, *A Regra Primitiva dos Cavaleiros Templários*, Lisbon, 1999.

GONÇALVES, Flávio, 'A legislação sinodal portuguesa da Contra Reforma e a arte religiosa' in *O Comércio do Porto*, Porto, 23 February 1960.

GONÇALVES, Flávio, 'Breve ensaio sobre a iconografia da pintura religiosa em Portugal' in *Belas Artes. Revista do Boletim da A.N.B.A.*, Lisbon, 2nd series, no. 27, pp 37-68.

GONÇALVES, Flávio, 'Inquisição Portuguesa e a arte condenada pela Contra-Reforma' in *Colóquio*, no. 26, Lisbon, 1963, pp 29-30.

GONÇALVES, Flávio, *História da Arte*, Lisbon, s.d.

GRAÇA, Luís, *Castle dos Templários*, Lisbon, 1994.

GRAÇA, Luís, *Convento de Cristo*, Lisbon, 1994.

GRAF, Gerard, *Portigal Roman*, 2 vols, Yonne, 1986–1987.

GUÉNON, René, *O esoterismo de Dante*, Lisbon, 1978.

GUÉNON, René, *O Rei do Mundo*, Lisbon, 1982.

GUÉNON, René, *Symboles de la science sacrée*, Paris, 1962.

GUIMARÃES, J. Vieira, Tomar, *Santa Iria*, Lisbon, 1927.

GUINGAND, Maurice; LANNE, Béatrice, *O Ouro dos Templários*, Lisbon, 1974; *Church of Santa Maria dos Olivais*, Journal of the Director General of Buildings and Monuments, nos 25–26, Lisbon, 1942.

KRAUTHEIMER, Richard, *Architettura Sacra Paleocristiana e Medievale*, Turin, Bollati Boringhieri, 1993.

KUBLER, Georges, *Portuguese Plain Architecture*, Middletown Wesleyan University Press, s.d.

KUBLER, George; SORIA, M., *Art and Architecture in Spain and Portugal 1500 to 1800*, Harmondsworth, 1959.

LACERDA, Aarão de (dir.), *História da Arte em Portugal*, vol. I, Porto, 1942.

LAMBERT, Élie, 'Remarques sur le plan des églises abbatiales de Tomar et de Batalha' in *Congresso do Mundo Português*, vol. II, Lisbon, 1940, pp 588-602.

LEITE, Ana Cristinap; PEREIRA, Paulo, 'Para uma leitura da simbólica manuelina' in *Prelo*, no. 5, Out.-Dez. 1984, pp 51-74.

LEITE, Ana Cristina; PEREIRA, Paulo, 'São João verde, o Selvagem e o Gigante em Gil Vicente – apontamento iconológico' in *Estudos Portugueses. Homenagem a Luciana Stegagno Picchio*, Lisbon, Difel, 1991.

LIZERAND, G., *Le Dossier de l'affaire des Templiers*, Paris, 1923.

MACHADO, P. S. de Lacerda, *Castle dos Templários, origem da cidade de Tomar*, Tomar, 1936.

MARKALE, Jean, *Histoire Sécrète de la France*, Paris, 1999.

MARKL, Dagoberto; BAPTISTA PEREIRA, Fernando António, *O Renaissance*, vol. VI of the *História da Arte em Portugal*, Lisbon, Publicações Alfa, 1986.

MARKL, 'Os ciclos: das oficinas à iconografia' in 'A pintura no período Manueline' in *História da Arte Portuguesa* (dir. Paulo Pereira), Lisbon, vol. II, 1995.

MATOS SEQUEIRA, Gustavo de, *Inventário Artístico de Portugal – Distrito de Santarém*, Lisbon, 1949.

MONTEIRO, João Gouveia, *Os Castles medievais portugueses*, Lisbon, 1999.

MORAIS, Francisco de, *Palmeirim de Inglaterra*, with preface to the edition by Rodrigues Lapa.

MOREIRA, Rafael, 'A arquitectura militar do Renaissance em Portugal' in *Actas do Simpósio sobre a introdução da arte da Renascença na Peninsula Ibérica*, Coimbra, Epartur, 1981, pp 281-305.

MOREIRA, Rafael, *A Arquitectura do Renaissance no Sul de Portugal*, Lisbon, 1991.

MOREIRA, Rafael, 'Arquitectura' in *Catálogo da XVII Exposição de Arte Ciência e Cultura do Conselho da Europa, Arte Antiga I*, Lisbon, 1983, pp 307-352.

MOREIRA, Rafael, 'A Ermida de Nª Sª da Conceição, mausoléu de D. João III' in *Boletim Cultural e Informativo da CMT*, no. 1, Tomar, 1981.

OLLIVIER, Albert, *Les Templiers*, Bourges, 1976.

PENNYCK, Nigel, *The ancient science of geomancy*, London, 1979.

PEREIRA, Paulo 'As grandes edificações' in *História da Arte Portuguesa* (dir. Paulo Pereira), vol. II, Lisbon, 1995.

PEREIRA, Paulo, 'Gil Vicente e a contaminação das artes' in *Temas Vicentinos. Actas do Colóquio em torno da obra de Gil Vicente*, Lisbon, Diálogo, 1992.

PEREIRA, Paulo, 'O Modo Gótico' in *História da Arte Portuguesa*, vol. I, Lisbon, 1995.

PEREIRA, Paulo, *A Obra Silvestre e a Esfera do Rei*, Coimbra, University of Coimbra, 1990.

PEREIRA, Paulo, *De Aurea Aetatis. A iconografia manuelina da west façade do Coro do Convento de Cristo em Tomar*, Lisbon, 2003.

PERNOUD, Régine, *Les Templiers*, Paris, 1974.

PERNOUD, Régine, *Les Templiers. Chevaliers du Christ*, Paris, 1995.

PONTE, Maria La-Salete, 'Abordagem arqueo-histórica dos Paços do Castelo dos Templários' in *Boletim Cultural e Informativo*, nos 11–12, Tomar, 1989.

QUADROS, António, *Introdução a uma estética existencial*, Lisbon, 1954.

QUADROS, António, 'Portugal, País Bernardino, Templário, Joaninno, Gralista e Paraclético' in *Les Templiers, le Saint-Esprit et l'Âge d'Or*, Lisbon, 1985.

QUADROS, António, *Portugal. Razão e Mistério*, 2 vols. Lisbon, 1986 (vol. I), 1987 (vol. II).

ROSA, Amorim, *História de Tomar*, vol. I, Tomar, 1965.

SANSONETTI, Paul-Georges, 'Da Távola Redonda à Esfera Armilar: Ideal cavaleiresco e domínio do Mundo' in *Cavalaria Espiritual e Conquista do Mundo*, Lisbon, I.N.I.C., 1986, pp 43-48.

SEBASTIÁN LOPEZ, Santiago, *Mensaje del Arte Medieval*, Málaga, 1984.

TEIXEIRA, Francisco Garcez, 'A Pintura Antiga da Church of São João Baptista em Tomar' in *Anais da União dos Amigos dos Monumentos da Ordem de Cristo*, vol. I, Tomar, 1933.

TEIXEIRA, Francisco Garcez, *Church of São João Baptista*, Tomar, s.d.

TEIXEIRA, Francisco Garcez, *O Tríptico da Vida de Cristo da Church of S. João Baptista*, Tomar, s.d.

TELMO, António, *História Secreta de Portugal*, Lisbon, Guimarães, 1977.

TOMÀS, Luís Filipe, 'L´idée impériale manuéline' in *La Découverte, le Portugal et l'Europe*, Paris, 1990, pp 35-103

TOURNIAC, Jean, *Melkitsedeq*, Paris, 1983.

VAN LENNEP, Jacques, *Alchimie*, Brussels, 1985.

VAN LENNEP, Jacques, *Arte y alquimia*, Madrid, 1978.

VITERBO, F. Sousa, *Dicionário Histórico e documental dos architectos, engenheiros e construtores portuguezes ou ao serviço de Portugal*, 3 vols, Lisbon, (1899–1922), facsimile edition, Lisbon IN-CM, 1988.